THE HEALER'S JOURNEY

Discovering the Healer Within You

SHARON J. LAND

LANDON
HALL
PRESS

Cover design by Jason Arias
Cover photo by Cos Lindstrom
Graphics by Stella Bellow, directed by Sharon Land

Published by Landon Hail Press
Paperback ISBN: 978-1-959955-09-2
Hardback ISBN: 978-1-959955-10-8

Content disclosure: This book explores themes around generational trauma, self-harm, suicide, narcissistic abuse, and addiction.

I dedicate this book to my parents, who brought me into this world, for always doing the best they could.
To the same who created the wound that allowed me to be truly birthed into this kaleidoscope of existence.
To my children, Emily Grace and Elizabeth Grace. You were created before my life was put together. Though you saw me broken, you also got to see me heal and alchemize every one of my experiences. You healed through your journey while I healed through mine. Thank you for unconditionally loving me and allowing the multifaceted expression of us all to be seen. You are the magic of the healers and healing we all need to see in this world.
To all of the angels who came into my life at the perfect time to help me see my mission through. I will never forget your kindness and empowerment.
May we all be open to experiencing freedom and love every moment of our Journey. May we all have seize the opportunity to be an angel to others along the way.

CONTENTS

THE HEALER'S JOURNEY

Prologue

The Beginning

His thought, "I'm coming," signals to me that he is near. But if he's more than a few miles away, he risks another nightfall before the arrival. A dangerous proposition. The curated energetic shield, created by his patron wizard, surrounds him. He trusts in the Divine light that has carried him from the hazards of darkness, despite sheer exhaustion and being gravely wounded.

It is a time when battles are fought regardless of truth. Fought because of duty and the will for control. Somehow, no matter how far any seeker travels, no matter how wounded or riddled with disease they are or on which side they fight, light always fills their journey to the tower. Without the light, the tower goes unnoticed.

They come with the expectation of healing, wholeness, and connection, of being understood and fully witnessed, which instills an eternal hope. He was no different. Our connection to our mission went beyond words and lifetimes carrying hope forward. This fervent hope is not in vain, this vision that their collective fight against darkness will bring societies to the light. That believing in a higher

1

level of art, spirituality, health, self-worth, and sacredness is their souls' true expression.

Worthy.

Radical acts to honor worthiness of all souls.

The tower is neutral.

I am neutral.

Christos is coming.

His energy is as unique as a fingerprint. I know by his cadence that he is limping, the gash above his left knee held together by a tourniquet. Feeling the full-bodied essence of his energy brings a smile from within.

We have known each other for lifetimes. In this one, he is the leader of Greek forces, but at his core, it is his connection to ancient mysticism and philosophy that drives his feet. I am again a healer, a mystic from the beginning of time, there to remember just this and to ascend beyond this.

One foot in front of the other, he moves forward. Carrying the vision of a world where darkness is understood, honored, and kept in check. His followers grow by the thousands.

Preparing the basin, I start channeling and open the portal.

He draws close to the tower. I am in the highest ascended and protected space. Once he arrives, I will run down the spiral stairs to greet him and bring him through another secret passageway, up to the Healing Tower. No one can know he is here. For all of our safety.

Serving in this capacity requires a precise understanding of the intricacies of this level of existence and service. I am well trained, practiced and known for maintaining this sacredness in energy, body, and physical space for others to heal.

My channel wide open, nothing is off the table when it comes to healing. My "senses," though, always start with my hands. They sometimes become almost too hot to endure, as the physical shape becomes amorphous, which is alarming to some, the first time they witness it. Guided from the light flowing through my crown and through my heart, the energetic veins of my hands grow and blossom into the perfect instrument and conduit.

Though I am all in in every way, there is a part of me that feels empty whenever he or others like him leave. Whether their stay be hours, days, or months, the afterward always requires me to recenter and ground back into my physical form. During this time, my heart always hurt, reminding me of my next level of growth. I know I am here for more. Never finished, yet still my own masterpiece of soul mastery and experience, nonetheless.

⸻ ●◦●◦● ⸻

As a child, I had a vision of the above and many others like this. Having grown up in a toxic family environment where I felt the opposite of valuable and talented, I stuffed both realities down into the metaphysical space I created within my physical body. The land of misfit parts and appearances. The place that held my conflict.

It wasn't until I met with different healers during my own seeking for transformation in this lifetime that, again, these visions came to life. Through their own channel.

I didn't think I'd ever had such an epiphany or that my heart of hearts held an experience like this one.

There is magic in connecting with aspects of our soul and mind that transcend all logic and reasoning. Time doesn't exist in this space. But it was in moments such as these when I was reminded how special we truly are. Despite whatever very painful and tangible experiences we go through in this and each lifetime, it is how we transcend through our own experiences that satisfies our soul and higher power.

Our souls and minds exist on a different plane and see a much bigger picture. Reaching this awareness will reveal the multi-lifetime existence and expression of your soul. You ascend any and all things by being in harmony with your physical expression now. Mind. Body. Energy. Spirit.

I am the healer's healer. You are a healer. I'm here to help you remember.

Welcome to *The Healer's Journey*.

INTRODUCTION

You may have found yourself here, reading this text, because you are at a crossroads, seeking a firmer foundation or definition of who you are or what your purpose is. You have lived an exceptional life and, in your journey, have transformed, achieved, and accomplished much. But you've not had a great deal of time to spend on parts yourself, because you have been focused on survival.

You might be more aware now of the influence of a narcissist, which, on some level, has informed your world about how others will try to define what is intrinsically within you. You may have come to the conclusion that, time and time again, that reflection is not coming from the thing that drives your purpose from within. Rather, it has become a reminder of how much you are misunderstood.

You know you have something in you that has kept you moving forward, despite the "failings or fallings." You somehow pick yourself up and carry on, because, despite how loud the voices have been outside of you, there is an inner voice coming from within you that has never left you.

You have withstood the traumas, the tragedy, and the suffering of this lifetime, because you know there is a purpose behind your existence, even though you don't always believe it or others can't see it.

There is a greatness in you that is waiting to come out. Even more than you have experienced or expressed to date. Despite the fact you have been exceptionally gifted and successful in your life, you seem to have done these things with your hands tied behind your back while metaphorically half blind. You need to know there is only one person like you who can do what you do in the way you were born to do it. You were born with a gift that, in many ways, your world was not ready to receive. There is nothing more devastating to the soul than to be in conflict with the world within you and around you.

You are either someone who has learned to seek your own source of power, who wants to know how, or who is ready to teach others how. You are done with old patterns and now want to learn how to live a life of alignment, ease, freedom, service, and wholeness. You are ready to know your own source of power and to drop the mask and show everyone the way up. You know that your greatest failing was not trying to pursue your full expression. To be a trailblazer means you must accept failing.

You are ready to take your next steps forward, letting the heavy cloak of your history fall gracefully to the floor. To let the full truth of yourself and who you are show fully.

You are a healer with a secret. You are exhausted, alone, and afraid to go forward. You have learned one of the fundamentals of life, that you alone must take care of yourself, and that you play the lead role and main character in every part of your journey. In your story.

Perhaps the heaviness of your secret has started to hijack your thoughts. Maybe your fears are showing up in your beliefs around what your success will require of you, and part of you is paralyzed to go on in the same way you have.

Yes, you are strong. Yes, you are a survivor. And furthermore, you have helped or saved many others in your life (and past lives). Yet somehow now, you secretly feel like you have failed in one or more areas and people in your life. Or, worse, failed yourself. You can't figure out why, if you have given your everything to everyone, like you were taught to do as a child, your life has been stopped in its tracks by disease. A crisis that, once any aspect of this is seen, it cannot be unseen.

Your thoughts say you are broken. *Why did it take so long? I'm behind.* Or even worse, *It's too late.* Not enough people are aware of the art and life force that is you.

Your own volcanic eruption is palpable. Sitting at your desk, lying in bed, driving your car, the tremor reminds you of its presence.

You have forgotten a divine and universal truth: *We are always whole, even when parts of us feel broken.*

Lesson number one: nothing in life is perfect other than divine truth and timing. So, if you have this book in your hands, you are right on time.

Now you must prepare for the greatest rising of your life.

Body, mind, spirit.

CHAPTER ONE

ARE YOU SURE IT'S ME?

"Healers are a unique type of people who utilize a form of lost magic, *potent* magic. From the Divine Source, each person is the instrument to allow this wisdom to flow. Each of us has our own expression of this universal form of magic. Just like each fingerprint is different, we each have our own experiences and are here to become a master of our own element or elements. To serve others."

You're probably asking yourself, How do I know I'm a healer? Well, I hope you know by now, based on your life's journey and the magic you have created out of seemingly nothing.

To experience and be a witness to you is akin to being sideswiped by a rare, unique (and possibly injured) bird in flight. Your magic lies within the truth your scars, though the journey from wound to scar is rarely available for others to see or fully appreciate. And those by whom you wish to be seen might find you invisible. You may not have the title *healer* or believe it is part of your job description.

I was recently at my youngest daughter's recording studio. Every Friday, I travel to New York City with her, where I find the creative energy of a buzzing recording studio the perfect place to sit and write. On that day, her mentor, a successful production engineer in the hip-hop industry, came to say hello.

"Hey, Mama Dukes! I hope you go up and watch one of the sessions your daughter is in now."

I begged off. "Thank you so much, but I am taking the time to write while she is in studio."

He looked puzzled. "What are you writing about?"

"I am writing my first book."

"Wow! What's it called?"

"*The Healers Journey.*"

We went back and forth for a while, and after a few more exchanges about it, he popped out, "Man, that is deeeeep," his voice punctuated with a rhythm as buzzy as the city streets. "You are really into this stuff, aren't you?" He laughed. "Man, you have definitely taken the red pill. This stuff is something I know nothing about."

I paused, took a breath in, embraced his energy, and then looked him squarely in his beautiful round brown face. With a warm smile, I whispered, "You are a healer, my friend."

His lion's mane of hair raised with his eyebrows and he looked even more puzzled. I don't think he knew what to make of me. Most don't. "Meeee? What makes you say that?"

Because I was in writing flow, I was already in a very open, tapped-in energy. I plunked into the unseen and channeled, "You have a gift of sound and sight. You see into the souls of others who are here to offer their own expression. You see and hear things others can or do not. You bring out and magnify the essence of who each artist is. You help them say what they need to say by seeing who they are. You make others feel seen and heard, and you help them to be seen and heard by others. That is one of the most healing things one can do for another. You most definitely are a healer. You have already helped my daughter to heal in infinite ways."

Then, there it was... The look I get often in my life. Awe, awkwardness, peace, discomfort, and love.

He softened from head to toe, his whole body relaxed, as he leaned over on the pool table. His smile brightened the room, and his teary eyes brought a reminder of the essence of the human spirit.

He mumbled, "Yeah, I guess I am. Huh. I never thought of myself like that. That's dope." After a hug, he walked away, and I think I heard him say, "I need to get my son to you. I would love for him to meet you."

Just like that, he was gone, and I was alone with the spirit of what was.

Just like this production engineer, you, too, may be blind to your own uniqueness, beauty, and gifts. Your success might be hidden deep within your physical, energetic, or emotional body.

Born pure, and without bias, prejudice, or confusion, you know what your needs are. Once our needs are responded to (or not responded to), this begins the journey of the healer. Your programming is cleverly camouflaged; more to come on that later. But know that your disarming grace is made with a touch of fragile magic and humility.

You never need to be perfect. You just need to be perfectly you.

Perhaps you are an agitator. You leave others part triggered, part aghast, excited, challenged, and inspired to consider the possibility of change in the pursuit of being exceptional. Exceptionally you.

Perhaps you are a dragon slayer, here to be the warrior to slay your own internal darkness. In truth, dragon slayers aren't here to bring death to anyone or anything. Their visit awakens the omnipotence of your inner verse. They protect the gateway to the collective's infinite capacity and earthly sanctuary.

Perhaps you are a combination of both and have the capacity to see, travel, move energy, heal, transmute, and transform. You know you are not here to usher others to the other side; rather, to find peace with being a soul within a human body. Knowing the universe's secret to bring heaven to earth. This is an enormous undertaking and usually requires an infinite amount of wisdom and embodiment of experiences.

One might feel heartbroken after a visit ends with any of the above, an understandable response to being witness to real-life magic.

If you have read this far and felt a stirring, you, my friend, are divine magic in motion, even on your weakest and most painful days. Realize you are here to experience all of this for a greater calling. To heal. The greatest gift, as described in many religious texts and orations.

Chances are you are a pivotal player in breaking your family's generational patterning. Without fear, you have placed your head in the mouth of a dragon to hear its secrets. This knowing creates the urge to grow deeper into your inner workings and to expand more greatly in your expression.

Most of all, you are from a long line of survivors. You are incredibly strong. Yet your greatest strength has become your greatest weakness.

At this stage, you may be aware of an energetic hum that's been with you all of your life. You might be confused about this. Or perhaps misunderstood or took it for granted. Whatever it is, the more you sit with the notion, the stronger the pull you have to go inward. You wish to seek answers about this thing that lives deep inside of you. How is it that, in the most challenging moments, its voice can be heard and wisdom sprays like a fountain of water?

The resistance to choose the inward journey can only be delayed for so long. At some point, you will lose the ability to choose. The universe is funny like that. It allows you the illusion of control for a time, until your divine time is called.

Everything is multifaceted magnetic energy. You are your own unique vibrational expression, and it is time for you to master your own element.

CHAPTER TWO

THE MIND

It was dark and not quite comforting. Actually, it felt "unwelcome," like the way an unexpected visitor might feel when they arrive at a party to which they were not invited. There was a constant ache vibrating from my heart and all around me. I felt unsafe. At times, I was panicked; at others, I was in waiting.

I saw myself in a cave with little food, water, light, or much stimulation. I sidled up to the walls that were weeping small amounts of water. Holding my mouth open, I would wait for a single drip to fall on my tongue, where it barely covered a fraction of it.

I remember tireless days spent working with my mind. When it grew to be too much, I would envision myself floating in the star-lined sky, held by the universe. Feeling the hum of the planets. Tethered to my suffering by a frayed bit of twine. I felt safe and free.

Focusing on the shining lights made me feel safe. It helped me feel that life made sense beyond the place to which I was tethered. Most of the time, I conserved my energy. I was never quite sure why, but I had a knowing that, soon, the day would come when I would need a significant amount of strength. Also, even more wisdom and power. I felt a patience beyond human existence. Patience fueled not by a waiting but by a knowing.

I longed for healthy connection, love, beauty, and creativity. I knew my mission would take me to a life far from this experience, and because my belief was that I was impermanent, I considered the potential for a new life a bonus. I knew in that moment, though, I wasn't ready.

I heard the words as I was called back into the cave. I anticipated not the desolation of that place, but the life I had been born to usher into existence. Until then, I would be patient.

For most of my life, I was told I was a good baby. I never cried, just ate and slept. It made sense, really. No one remembered much about me from when I was little. My first steps, teeth, words, or even my most memorable and traumatic experiences were seen, heard, felt, and remembered only by *me*.

I learned at an early age that I was good if I didn't need anything, and I was bad if I needed anything.

It was as though the space I occupied was borrowed, and at any minute, it would be taken back, and I'd be bumped out of the queue.

I learned new ways to feel fulfilled. I found interesting methods to find ways to attune. Swinging and humming took up much of my day.

The door lock on our house was depressed as soon as I went outside; my vivid memories of trying to get back in for any reason still send panic to the pit of my gut.

I got the same sensation the time my foot slipped on the narrow cement wall and I fell flat on my stomach, while trying to enter the side door of our home, which, at times, my mother would forget to lock. I learned that day what it felt like to have the wind knocked out of me. But beyond that, I learned my capacity for survival. I had just tried the door, and, at age seven, I was beside myself. Both of my feet slipped out from underneath me, and my head, sternum, and stomach broke my fall.

I lay there with my face on the six-inch-wide concrete wall, trying to stay calm. I couldn't see or breathe. My superpower kicked in, and I froze everything.

It was fifteen to thirty seconds before I attempted to breathe. Then, my instincts kicked in. I slowly exhaled, emptying my lungs. Then, I inhaled a sip of air, exhaled, and emptied before inhaling a tiny sip. I repeated this several times, until I slowly found my rhythm. I felt a faint hum. Something chanted and hummed beyond my physical space; it was breathing, too. We were breathing together. I found myself buzzing, a vibration deep within my sternum.

At seven years old, this second eruption had planted in me a seed of consciousness. I was reminded I had a tether to something greater than me. The first awakening was created in the womb through a combination of best intentions by my overwhelmed mother. Trauma is felt and stored as soon as life begins.

Unable to see, I pushed myself to sitting and waited. Lights flitted across the darkness, and somehow, I felt calm.

There is something that happens when we experience difficulties, trauma, or challenging circumstances. We learn about our own capacity to survive. Our reptilian brain, which has transcended lifetimes, activates. This creates something called cognitive achievement, the equivalent of mental acuity. It's the thing in our brains that informs us of calculations based on perceptions created by our own experiences. It's the thing that talks us though the seemingly impossible. Our neuro-patterning exists in clusters, and our pathways can be blocked by unrepaired trauma.

Though armed forces re trained how to handle war and conflict when it happens, some experience the battle when they are placed in it, *knowing* they are in over their head; something in their bodies signals that death is imminent death. Others see the possibilities for survival. This positive perception makes the difference between life or death. What makes the difference between the two responses?

A perceived threat also can trigger or activate our reactions, affecting our free will, even when there actually is no danger. For instance, Navy SEALs, in their training, must do deep-sea dives. They train for hours prior to going into the deepest, blackest part of the sea. For some, panic is triggered when they are deep underwater, subject to the great pressures of the sea. A part of their brain (the basal ganglia) tells the body there is a threat. And the individual is compelled to rise to the surface too quickly, despite all their training and the warnings not to. As a result, many trainee divers may encounter serious threat to health and safety, which, without swift treatment, can be life-threatening. This while other SEAL trainees correctly remain below, completely unaware of this panic reaction, as they themselves do not experience the cognitive activation that tells them there is danger.

Why did you think this happens? I, for one, know that our experience creates the intelligence of our body, mind, and spirt, and we get to turn this intelligence into wisdom. Wisdom is the embodiment of our existence. Our state of being. It occupies our body, mind, and energy and is driven by our soul and highest self.

Healers have innate wisdom, derived from experiences that develop our intelligence. Ascended healers transmute information into gold.

I first remembered my experience in the womb through an inner-child/soul healing. It was like a homecoming. I cried cathartic tears, remembering the conditions of my mother's womb: feeling unwelcome, overwhelmed, stressed, and starved, surrounded by hostility.

I later learned from my mother that, when she was pregnant with me, she was a new mother to my colicky few-months-old sister, in a troubled, explosive, and unpredictable marriage, and had been ordered by her doctor to lose weight while carrying me. So, carrying ahead on doctor's orders, she lost over thirty pounds.

My first trauma in this lifetime was in the womb. Learning that, it all made so much sense. And without knowing any details of this experience, I knew it was true, because I had spent a lifetime repatterning the same energy. Until I greeted it, understood how it affected me in my present-day life, and healed it. This experience was not just something I stored in my brain; it echoed in my nervous system.

This is the power of healing. It took over forty years for me to arrive back at that particular moment (decades ago) and to find a loving shaman. But it was the love I discovered of myself that led me to a greater love within me. There is so much magnificence in this world when you rise above your own suffering. We truly can heal any and all things.

Getting to this part of your journey is a feat that your soul and God (Universe, Source, Goddess, Gods, Divine: please insert whatever resonates with you) know and understand. You will meet instruments of the divine along the way that will collapse time for you. The more you journey onward, however, the more places you will visit and the more parts of your soul you will meet.

———————————•◦●◦●◦●◦•———————————

CHAPTER THREE

THE BODY

We are fascinated with books like *The Body Keeps Score* and *Medical Medium*, along with all the enlightening information at our disposal that offer us new insights or perhaps old wisdom, all at the perfect time. All information we receive is designed to help us align with our physical, emotional, spiritual, relational, and collective health. But without the physical embodiment (see the root of this word) of any information, we are just a head floating around and over our body.

Knowledge is at complete disconnect from wisdom. Even when you're struggling, you are aware of the struggle and unaware of the ways to connect back to a sense of wholeness. We usually seek these resources at a time we are experiencing something that now cannot be ignored.

Then why do most people struggle or even stop working after they complete the initial stages of addressing whatever issue has come up? After the "emergency signals" seem to subside?

Pain. What some wrestle with is the fact that their survival skills (via chemicals released in our bodies), which are designed to maneuver us through a temporary situation in their lives, have numbed the pain receptors designed to keep us *healthy*. Once those survival chemicals subside, pain resurfaces, and usually to a greater degree than ever before. So, what do our vibrational bodies do? Trick us into releasing the numbing dissociative chemicals again. The longer the time frame and cycle, the greater the potential to damage our tri-phasic bodies.

My teeth were buzzing. I'd just received another jolt from the electric fence, a thin wire twisted around a plastic-coated hook that looked like a bread-bag tie. It was the mid-1970s, and most things didn't come with safety labels, especially not the old electric fence at a horse farm.

I had heard the owner of the farm, Mr. Audley, say he'd had to increase the voltage of the fencing around the big pastures. We called it "the back forty." (For years, I had no idea what that meant. Later, I learned it meant *forty acres*; a valuable resource in the state of New Jersey.) What I did know was that the back forty became my metaphysical training ground and a safe space for the magical formative years of my young life.

One or more of the horses learned they could withstand the jolt of the fence in pursuit of their version of a jail break. I always imagined it was the sourest of our lesson horses, Buddy. But I was wrong. I learned the breakout was actually led by Silhouette, an older, semi-arthritic mare. She'd plow right through until the wire broke.

Silhouette was a former high-end show horse whose injuries prevented her from competition. She had been retired from major competition and become a lesson horse, but before she did, she had been shoulder to shoulder with some of the best, her life's purpose fully expressed. Nowadays, she appeared dull and unfazed by most things. Maybe she was numb; but maybe she was resolved, content, and fulfilled. Whatever her state, one thing was certain: I underestimated her in most ways.

By the time I met her when I was seven years old, she was a shadow of her former self, a perfect juxtaposition, her slim filly whose glory days were winding down, and I was a chubby girl who was just beginning to see the world outside of my home life. She was a being who had seen it all and had found home anywhere she was sent. I had no context other than my parents.

When the break happened, the herd walked, trotted, cantered out of the pasture, completely free, and then... they all went right to their stalls. A funny thing about herds: once formed, they stay together.

I learned to listen for the whistle as my trainer, Nancy, called to her seven dogs. It was a sing-songy, thin, high-low high-low whistle. The sound was quite different from her otherwise larger-than-life persona, so it always caught me by surprise and made me smile.

My trainer wore jeans with a leather belt that had a big buckle. In the summer, she added a tank top, and in winter, big, bulky coats. And she was always dusty, no matter the time of year.

Whenever I looked at her, I felt a terrible pain in my hands and stomach. Sometimes, I'd get dizzy and my vision would narrow into a pinpoint. Sometimes during the years I knew her, the sensations were stronger than others. Though I always knew this was not something actually happening within me, something I had to worry about, I had to learn that this "signal" was coming from her specifically.

I later discovered that Nancy had diabetes that she struggled to keep regulated at times. One year, my mother casually revealed this to me when she told me about making her a "diabetic cake." I also learned to connect this feeling to my sensing diabetes in others.

After her whistle, she would bellow for me and my sister to meet her in the barn with the horses. We usually found them hanging out in one another's stalls, the equine equivalent of a slumber party. As soon as our trainer arrived, she broke up the party and enlisted us to help return each horse to their own stall. As they were led to their stalls, their personalities shined through. Some of the horses would pin their ears back, while others pranced and whinnied. They all seemed full of themselves for pulling one over on us, like an inside joke among them. I felt a sense of belonging to this barn, one of the first times in my life I tangibly felt held in a space.

To lead a horse, we were taught to loop a rope over their neck, which was hardest for me, as the smallest, so I would usually get bumped, stepped on, or dragged by one animal or another. Other hazards included possibly being slammed into a door jam or trapped in a stall. I did my best to keep the horses safe and myself alive.

When I did get hurt, I soon learned to keep it to myself, as our trainer would not be happy about it. It would mean I had done something wrong. She might tell my mother, who would get angry because I had made her look bad. I had already learned at this young age that no one around me would make my hurts feel better *and* I'd suffer double punishments. The lesson was for me to deal with the pain alone.

They say the best training is prevention rather than correction. I'd have to agree. But I'd say pain became my greatest teacher.

I mostly wore hand-me-downs from my sister, and nothing ever fit quite right. The waist of my pants always too tight, and my shirt was never long enough to cover my bulging belly. No matter what I wore, however, my nine-year-old self knew more than most adults about the reality of horse training, things I learned through trial and error.

When I was nine or younger, my sister and I were dropped off to work at the barn on most weekends. The drive there along the old country roads was always full of tension. My mom took most turns on two wheels of her White Jeep, a car that was missing a bench seat in the back, so my sister and I had to sit on the wheel well of the "bumpy car."

I didn't know any other way, nor did I care. We were going to the closest thing to heaven that I knew, partly because it was away from home, but mostly because I was given full autonomy to work as a barn hand.

So, as my teeth buzzed and I brought myself back from shock, I placed the electric fence into its holder and ventured out into the field. The back forty was rough and rocky, filled with tufts of hard grass on the barn-facing side. But just past the trees, the field opened into a magic kingdom. Nothing short of Heaven on Earth to me. Though I might get in trouble for going out there by myself, the punishment was a lesser pain than the one of regret. I felt called to go into the field and to be with the fourteen or so horses that were my mentors.

First, I saw the draft cross gelding, Domino. He was one of the herd leaders and was standing off in the distance with two others, watching their surroundings. Two heads popped up. Ears like radars turned their opening in my direction. I stopped walking, took a deep breath to quiet my excitement and anxiety. As I did, they lowered their heads and munched on the green grass, turning their ears toward me, then away, and then toward me again as I approached.

The sweet smell of honeysuckle overwhelmed my nose, and something else in my senses awakened. More than a sixth sense. I could "hear" some of the instincts of the herd. At first, I recoiled from the experience and felt uncomfortable in the void where the communication once was. I was being guided toward the other side of Domino, where much of the herd stood. The two guards nodded their heads as their relaxed bodies meandered to the other side of Domino. Were they leading me? No... That could not be.

One broke away, and the other, George, who was in clear channel with me, sauntered closer to a bunch of four. Facing the four, George pinned his ears and straightened his neck. The four began moving their feet, grabbling mouthfuls of grass as they traversed slowly. I noticed they didn't run away. They moved in an arc shape and started to come back toward my direction.

I stopped in my tracks, wondering what I should do. I was in the middle of the field with zero protection or place to run. Nimbus looked toward me with his soft eyes. The first of four, Nimbus continued the arc and walked directly in front of me then away, as he continued his arc to the left. The others followed him. Rather than think, I felt into the experience and willed them to circle around me. My heart was overflowing with awe and love for my equine family and this exchange. To my surprise, on the next circle, Nimbus walked behind me, and the others followed.

This time, rather than keep my eyes averted, I smiled and looked at Nimbus. His pace increased. Lifting up his head, he signaled to the others to pick up their energy, and they matched his cadence. I tilted my head back with an even bigger smile. Caught up in the moment, I continued to play with my emotions and body, curious how this change would potentially alter the change within them. This was not a coincidence, and I wanted to test the theory.

Crouching down to hold my feet, I made my body small and looked out of the side of my eyes at the group. I was shocked when they slowed to a stop. I felt their energy shift as Nimbus turned to face me. The others followed suit again. "Is this really happening?"

Keeping my eyes fixed on Nimbus, I slowly stood, and his back legs pivoted his body to walk on. The others followed. I was beaming, buzzing, and tuned into a frequency that felt like home. It wasn't the first I'd experienced this. I knew it, but I just couldn't put my mind to when I had felt this before.

In the distance, I heard the high-low, high-low whistle of my trainer calling her dogs, signaling it was the end of her day, which meant my mother was coming soon. Taking a few quick steps away to start my run, I stopped and turned around to my family.

"Thank you for teaching me," I said and ran for the fence line to find the gate.

Chapter Four

The Soul

I was sitting in my car as her voice boomed through the speakers. My ancient soul smiled, seeing how "modern inventions" mirrored mysticism.

I was on my way to a store that sold home decor, candles, and tchotchkes. Anyone who knows me well understands my disdain for clutter and mismatched bits. I was mentally preparing myself for the store when my youngest daughter, Lizzy, called. This had become rare over the past four years. Not my mindlessly walking the aisles alone! That happened often, especially when I was numbing the pain of my daughter not wanting to see or talk with me for over a year. And I understood why she hadn't, which made it hurt even more.

Like any parent, when my child called, I answered. But in my case, whenever *she* called, it set off an indescribable chain of events in my body. She was sixteen or less at the time, and we hadn't lived together for a few years.

We had been through hell and back, psychological and physical torture by my second husband, whom I brought into our home. We had lived in this torture, fighting the fight for our lives and for the liberation of our souls. She hadn't liked him from the beginning. That, coupled with her energetic sensitivities and less-than-mainstream presentation, made her an easy target for him to attack covertly. She and Emily saw me go from being independent, self-sufficient, and overly loving to a mere shell of my former self. Recovery from this has taken years for all of us, and it will continue for years to come. Healing trauma from sociopathic abuse is a hard road.

The marriage and relationship lasted for three years: the tension, abuse, survival, and shame became blankets that covered us in our own confusion and tucked us in at night. To me, these feelings were so familiar. During my healing journey, I learned how deeply they travel. I have been carrying this energetic patterning for lifetimes. And later, I learned that my ancestors, too, had carried their similar unhealed patterns for lifetimes. I was aware of the pain I felt, being a child of generational trauma and unhealed wounds, so I very much wanted to spare my own children the same. I was well-intended but misguided by false programming.

It was hard to accept what happened during those three years. The abuse was like a gaping hole left by a meteor impacting both of my children, and the process to heal all this into a scar has been my heaviest lift thus far. It has been my misguided journey toward love, on a path paved with humility, pain, and truth.

The metaphysical and energetic chords that connect a mother and daughter are palpable. I can reach out and pluck them, hearing their tune and feeling their unique vibration.

As an intuitive, the experience of the senses is overwhelming at times. But slaying these internal dragons for fifty years prepares you for almost anything. And the divine connection to our children goes beyond preparing.

My daughter Lizzy experienced the same divine gifts. We spoke of it telekinetically and in 3-D. When she was fourteen, she learned how to throw energy. Hers was piercing and disarming, the closest feeling to a ball of energy the size of the moon's love in 4-D form. At times, our knowing was the only thing that kept us from floating completely away from our connection.

We were at an appointment where she was receiving a metaphysical healing. Her friend had come along. Lizzy lay on the table, and her friend left to get a slice of pizza down the street.

As Lizzy lay there, about to receive her own healing, she felt her friend suddenly feel sad and alone. Lizzy tossed a ball of energy directly to her friend just as she was entering the pizzeria.

Later, on the drive home, her friend told Lizzy about the experience, and Lizzy told her that she was, in fact, the one who did it. She recounted some of the feelings and thoughts her friend was having, and after a moment of "*Oh my Gods*" and "*Mom!*" I smiled.

She and I discussed her gifts often. I wanted her to know that her superpowers are good, real, and best used when she herself raises her own vibration. For a teenager suffering from codependency and trauma bonding, this is a tough concept to accept and understand, but she always wanted to use her gifts to help others.

Even though there was a time she cut me off from seeing her, I knew she was continuing to learn how to work with her energetic veil when I could no longer sit on my couch at home, tuning into her and simultaneously blowing out skunk-like smoke from my mouth, knowing exactly what she was doing and how she was feeling. She was shocked and giddy to know about this, when I told her. She put a pin in the topic for future discussion. She taught herself alone how to build the iron curtain of protection from my seeing. Pretty powerful for a novice, but again not surprising.

So, I wasn't completely shocked, when I answered the phone, that I could hear fear in her voice. I could tell she was worried. I wondered if it was because she had realized how long she had gone without touching base with me, or maybe it was because she was in a tough spot. I wasn't sure, but I knew that I best served her by being as neutral as possible and allowing her to tell me what she needed in this moment.

My default in these moments was to get chatty and to find something to talk about that was the opposite of the elephant in the room. The funny thing is, I'm not like that in any other part of my life or with most people I know. But with my daughters, it is hard to be direct. I know how much I have hurt them, so I yield to them and to their journey, while at the same time I don't always know what they have healed, themselves. Or which timeline they might be coming from. How long they have been drinking the Kool-Aid from *The Matrix*, from their father.

Somehow, we landed on a discussion about something I had shared with a client recently. They had said, "Gosh, your children are so lucky to have you as their mother. You are so open-minded and loving and kind."

My client's words had activated a spot in my deeply furrowed roots that writhed in pain. I could literally hear the crackling of the wooden resin that, like a casket, contained this secret as they writhed. I could feel the familiar wrestle between tension and movement, with struggle giving way to a hopeful existence.

"Lizzy," I reassured my client, "others, including my closest family, do not think like that at all." I leaned in on my humor in order to distance myself from my pain. I said, "My girls are writing a book about me, and it isn't about what a good mother I was."

Most of my clients also knew this type of pain. The thing that got me through was holding a vision of my future self, being with my children in safe quarters and celebrating our individual journeys, our souls rising into purpose. I paused when I realized that, today, we were further away from the original wounding and closer to the vision than we ever had been.

Our healing is a continuous spiral that threads throughout our lives. We help others most when we share from our truth, which transmutes any past wounds to wisdom. You serve well when you remove the mask of illusion and show the wisdom of your scars after they've healed.

Telling this story to Lizzy was one part confession, one part taking further responsibility, and one part speaking my truth into the universe. I would not continue to hide behind my hurts as part of my identity. My heart and arms were open, ready to receive, whatever she had to say. I was trying to create a healthy dynamic in a life full of nothing but.

A bucketload of our ancestors' guilt, abuse, shame, and discontent came tumbling out of their baskets like starving beggars looking for food, not realizing that each one of us was the key to our own healing. Our own nourishment was to be found in turning our own pain into thriving.

"Mom. Stop. I don't want you to say that. Or think that. *Ever*. Because it's not true. You are a *good* mother. You are the kindest, *most* loving, and incredible human being I know. You are so powerful and strong and magical. I'm so unbelievably proud that you are my mother. I can't believe how strong you are, even when you seem the most fragile. It just hurts to be with you. I'm working on that."

I love you but it hurts to be with you

I love you but it hurts to be with you

Once we are deep into our own healing, we can "see" through the omnipresent metaphysical eye. This eye can see the root cause of all wounds. I could see this ancestral pattern clearly in my daughter in that moment, and still, it hurt so much.

This was evidence of intergenerational trauma being played out in the vibrational patterning of both of us. I was doing my best to break it. There was a reason our two souls were reflecting this to each other. If we are experiencing this, it is validation that others are, as well. Each of those souls is being directed with a purpose to bring change to the Earth through transmutation of our own challenges. I took a sip of water to wash the taste of blood from both of our ancestors' wounds out of my mouth.

Those words, "It hurts to be with you," from my fifteen-year-old created a chain reaction within me of full-body and soul sobbing. I knew that souls dating seven generations back collectively sobbed through my physical body. The vibration expressed as an ache, a reminder to me that I am merely the instrument.

Love hurts. I had done enough healing to know *that* is a lie.

What a lie!

Love *heals.*

Love lives and breathes between wisdom and truth.

I knew the best thing I could do was to continue on my own healing journey and pray for hers.

I sat alone in my car as her voice boomed around me. And the sounds of a concert of memories: as I birthed her; and of the whispers of the trees as she and her sister, Emily, walked along the river on the Colombia Trail, as I saw both of them talking to their guides. I knew then I was bearing witness to something special. I had no idea this was their initiation to their healing to become healers.

I had said enough. She had said enough. Yet there was so much more to say. My heart twisted, and a steady stream of tears poured from my eyes. But these were solely mine to know and not hers to see. Even in our darkest days, I always trusted that Lizzy would rise into her gifts no matter what.

My daughters and I shared a traumatic bonding that goes back for hundreds of years in our family. It is a deep connection and understanding, blocked by a poison in our collective programming and system. A thousand false truths. Each of us has the antidote, but few have found the key. The evidence was clear by looking at our ancestors' experiences. *Damnit. Damnit.* All roads lead to this. Every life we have lived, two solitary lines. All of them now intersect. Love hurts. Now, we get to change this for ourselves.

The smallest moments can and will change your life. Sometimes, you know it in the moment. Other times, you see it when you are further on your climb toward your spiral staircase of ascension.

This was one where I felt the shift right there in the moment. Through my own self-healing, I learned:

Divine wisdom and the opportunity to change our trajectory don't always feel good to receive. In those moments where it *realllly* hurts, we need to lean on faith. Faith outstretches our arms to the unknown and what is possible. This possibility is the key to our success. And the path toward this comes from our daily practice. It is where our true foundation solidifies and creates a place for our miracles to be held. Our daily practice of self-healing and mastery is a place where we come to know the multiple sensations of how the divine communicates with us. It is then that we can understand all that lives within us. Some belong, and others are metabolized and let go. We can remove right from wrong, good from bad, and call ourselves up to embody our truth. This is true love.

Love Liberates.

When this liberation occurs, we can then create the opportunity to feel compassion for others. This faith creates a practice of patience and compassionate distance. When this liberation occurs within you, it is up to you. I chose this decades ago, in 2005, when I started my biggest pivot to heal from a stroke. It has taken this long for me to bring this now to you.

On the boat ride from the shores of Italy to Ellis Island, where my great-grandfathers arrived. In my great-great-great-grandmother supporting her family through her own intense physical disease. In my paternal grandmother being chased through the house by her husband as he shouldered a loaded shotgun, my father witnessing. In my grandfather, who not-so-silently suffered with mental illness and made several failed suicide attempts. It's all there, and if it isn't healed, it will be here in our present.

Through it all, every one of them was forced to survive incredible trauma. They masked themselves to summon "success," so their future generations wouldn't suffer, all while silently hoping something outside of them would answer the begging of their own souls to be freed. To have each of their lives turned into something good. They all had varying degrees of their own knowing of health; they all did the best they could. Instead of healing through magic. Alchemy. Hope. Healing. Empowerment. They repeated what had kept them alive: numbing, magnified emotions, aggression, and suffering.

In my own daily practice, I declared out loud, "This is where it will end. No more suffering!"

Turning my attention to my daughter on the phone, I said, "Thank you for being so full if grace. Thank you."

I was left sitting in a pool of forgiveness that had started as a tiny seed of healing years ago, followed by three years of gutting trauma by deconstructing a tsunami of false truth in a myriad of alternative and holistic ways. One loving step at a time.

This was ancestral trauma. Generational trauma and strength wrapped in a bow. I had learned that mental illness, physical disease, and detachment from our highest self comes from a framework of unhealed trauma. The seeds had been planted. *And* this was my purpose. Healing all of it. Life in the quantum gives us a glimpse of our interconnectedness, multiverse-style. One timeline multiplied by the infinite measure of time. Once you can feel what you can't see, you lean in to the unknown even more.

———————•●◆●•———————

Chapter Five

Medical Medium

The first time I consciously remember understanding the unique energy of physical disease and what it felt like to be a healing conduit was when I was seven years old. It sounds weird to say it that way, but I know it isn't *just me* who heals. *I have always been a divine instrument of the universe.*

The time I suffered most was when I tried to run from my higher power and abandon the parts of myself that were a conduit.

I was at an old equestrian facility that was full of English riding horses, chickens, goats, and dogs. I was kicking a stone down the path to a paddock when I was overcome by the taste of iron on my tongue. A part sour and part full-bodied taste of old pipes took over my mouth before it filled with an abundance of saliva.

I raised my eyes from the stone touching my foot and I focused on a horse in a small paddock up and to the right. I slowly approached it like a magnet being summoned. While my mouth still signaled, I felt my hands grow hot. It was the type of burn you feel at the extremes of either heat or cold.

My hands led the way. As I grew close, my hands traveled inward beyond the horse's skin and could "see" an internal mass on his shoulder. There was blood building around a frayed, chord-like substance.

I reached my hands through the splintered boards. His ears pinned as he shifted his weight away and then returned to within inches of my swollen fingers. The longer I stayed, holding my hands inches from his wound, the stronger my heartbeat, and I felt pure love pour from my fingertips.

He lowered his head, and his eyes softened. I faintly recall feeling like we were both inside an ambient group of pirouetting circles.

As he discharged a blob of liquid from his lips into a large puddle on the ground, I jolted. My mother was yelling my name. "Sha-*ronnnnn.*"

And just like that, it was over, and I was running to both my mother and sister, who were sitting in our white Jeep Scout. I hopped in the back of the "bumpy car," and the engine revved while climbing the hill away from the farm. Peering out the back window as I opened and closed my swollen hands, I watched my four-legged friend grow smaller as we drove away.

I continued to have more experiences just like that one. In them, there was no differentiation between any living being, although I recognized an entity that showed me the way toward an inner conflict, whether it was a medical disease, mental illness, or turmoil, a spiritual disturbance or a tortured soul.

It took me decades to understand that these experiences were not unique to me, but they were shared by most of those by whom I was surrounded. I saw that God and the universe allowed me to experience these senses in this way because this was part of my destiny, and the experiences were the paving stones to my service here on Earth. But first, I needed to understand the spiritual laws that accompanied this ability, because it is a responsibility. These lessons came in hard, fast, and copiously. Most of the energy I needed to understand was my own resistance to this powerful force within me and to how painful it was, being the only one I knew who lived the way I did.

Only you are like you. Only you possess what you bring. What you have, people need. What you see, others need you to see.

I would see black particles coming from out of people's mouths, and rather than follow them as they drifted into thin air, I would travel down to where they came from, to their origins, which was not always where they settled.

I'd always know where to go. I could feel, see, send, and hear what others could not. I could see things as a spirit who communicated with me the same way a visitor would, through all the ways we communicate and beyond.

I sensed shadows in the throat, glue-like substances in the breast, a humming hurt in the liver, and disoriented disjointed spirits in the brain. I saw visitors from past lives, plus abuse and unresolved trauma, all represented by a unique energetic impression revealed through auditory, multi-sensory expressions.

Once, I made a mistake and spoke with my father about what I saw. I was ten or eleven years old at the time, and my sister was twelve. "Sheryl" was one of my mother's friends from work, and she would come to parties at our home occasionally.

"Is she okay?" I asked my father, even though my question didn't make sense logically, because she was a very kind and warm person. "I think she's sick. Every-time I think about her, I feel nauseous."

My father dismissed me by giving me a look and saying, "You are being disrespectful." Which was his usual way of avoiding anything uncomfortable. Then, without hesitation, he went back to reading the paper.

I feared my father. He had a powerful presence, one of intense anger, sadness, and distance plus a penchant for being unpredictable. He had a laugh that boomed and a singing voice that broke hearts. He always struck me as distant during most of my younger years. It was hard to see that he, too, had suffered from intense emotional and physical abuse when he was younger.

At times he would come into my room after his outburst and share some of his experiences as a child. He weighed over 200 pounds in fifth grade, was the youngest of three, and his father, to my best surmising, would be diagnosed as bipolar with major depressive episodes. My father shared that his childhood had been difficult, and he was thankful for his then teacher, our now Aunt Lois, who was his champion in many ways.

Through the years, I learned that his father, my biological grandfather, used material objects and psychological torture as his means to power and control.

When my father was a young adult, his father had many suicide attempts (which he to this day has not discussed with me), and my father was the one called or went for help.

It was through both him and my mother I learned to let my emotions build to an uncontainable level. Though his was less frequent than my mother's physical abuse, he would hit me so hard with his hand, it left welts on my bare bottom. Once, he grabbed me by the neck and jacked me up onto the wall, repeatedly slamming my back and head into the basement wall. He screamed while my feet dangled, helpless.

I went into complete shock. I left my body, as I usually did, and completely checked out. Barely registering the fact that my friend and her father were there, witnessing the whole thing.

My father continued to further distance himself from us, especially me, while my mother increased the level of emotional abuse she meted out, in turn adding to my pain. I was relieved not to be seen by him during those times when he checked out. At other times, I was utterly confused by his inconsistent position, for example, pretending he was my hero when he came into my room at night and said, "Your mother doesn't love you as much as she does your sister." Or when he talked about the bullying I experienced at school, somehow making it about himself.

I could see him watching out of the corner of his eye whenever my mother spat out the words, "Fat, dumb, rotten brat," or when she slapped my face or hit me with a brush or wooden spoon in response to her frustration at my failure to comply with the ever-changing rules and expectations in our household. Having this as my normal, as a child, created programming that formed my identity as my abusers' secret-keeper.

<hr>

My parents were amateur actors and singers in plays at the high school where my mother worked. And my sister and I often watched them perform. During one of those shows, as he sang in *Fiddler on the Roof*, I saw for the first time how deeply wounded my father's soul was. His tenor pulled at our collective heartstrings, and I felt everyone's body levitate as he poured it all out for us. My soul wept.

As it did, I "received" an abundance of chatter and downloads, which, at that point, I was already used to. But one in particular became my focal point. It was coming from their friend, Sheryl, who was clearly suffering.

She was in the play. Her oxygen levels were low, and her heart felt bittersweet, because she had such great love in her life. She was on stage in a supportive role, but her feminine energy was closed off. Her breasts were riddled with disease, much more so than the last I time I'd seen her. Darkness wrapped around her eyes and throat.

I had already learned my lesson about speaking up, so I sat quietly in my seat while watching it all unfold. She later was diagnosed with breast cancer. Although she received treatment, she ultimately lost the fight. Her body went back to the earth, and her soul was set free.

When I was ten years old, this experience was beyond difficult for me to fully grasp. I had no idea the empowerment that God/Universe/Source energy was providing me, because it was muddied by my chronic abuse at home. Abuse never stays in one place. It travels and bleeds into all other parts of our lives. At school, I was bullied, and while I'm sure I wasn't an easy child to get along with, most people would describe me as "nice."

Around that time, I also started to have vivid nightmares. They were consistently the same: a man trying to kill me. In the nightmare, I knew him. I'd hear him say, "It's okay, honey pie."

He showed up in the shadows, no matter where I was. He was always there when I was alone in my bed, and I would run screaming for help, looking for someone to help me. But no one ever surfaced. I'd run away, arching my back as he swung an axe and attempted to sever the base of my spine. Sometimes, I would hit the floor, waking me up; other times, I woke in my bed, breathless and covered in sweat, my back knotted with a Charlie horse, an intensely painful contraction, while my throat was on fire and my voice hoarse from screaming. I was petrified to fall asleep again.

An uncanny thing happened one day while I was home. I was working on my homework, and my mother was on her way home from teaching. The phone rang and I sprang into action and ran down the hallway to answer.

My sister and I had an unspoken competition around most things, and answering the phone was one of them. In our usual performance, we collided in the kitchen doorway and both pushed each other through the door. I had no intention of hurting her; it was just to set her back enough to win the phone-answering championship. This time, I won.

After grinning at my sister, I directed my attention to the phone. "Hello?" I said after picking it up.

After three seconds of silence, I heard a man's voice say, "Sharon. Hello, honey pie. Don't hang up. Let me talk to you, honey pie." It was *him*.

I pulled the hot phone away from my ear. It was the man in my nightmares. My lower back seized up, and my mouth suddenly went dry.

I could feel his presence, just like in my dreams. The smell of his leathery, weathered skin filled my nostrils, and I slammed the phone down. I stood there, dumbstruck and terrified, still holding the receiver.

Then I felt my hand vibrate as the phone rang again. I lifted it again to my ear and, to my utter disbelief, it was him again. I went completely mute as he breathed in the phone. "Honey pie. Don't hang up, Sharon."

This happened two more times over the next few years. The nightmares visited me randomly, and I'd wake the same way every time: terrified. My young mind wondered how someone from my dreams could cross over into my waking days. Also, no one ever saved me in my dream. And no one ever acknowledged that they heard me screaming in my sleep.

At the same time, my ability to "see" illness and disease became stronger. Every part of my experience became clearer; the visions, tastes, smells, dreams, messengers, and divine guidance all grew stronger. In all honesty, I still can't list how I experience this fully. As I become a healthier vessel, it, too, becomes deeper, wider, and more powerful. Anything about someone's conflict, from spiritual ascension, life span developmental issues, relational conflicts, etc., I was "given" this information about them.

I also started experiencing my own mystery illnesses as a young child. I would have excruciating pains in my stomach, migraines so strong that the blood vessels in my eyes would burst, and I experienced sheer exhaustion. I was seen by many specialists, and although they didn't get to the root cause (trauma), they treated my symptoms.

I usually followed their medical advice until I hit a dead end. Then, intuitively, I would start to shift and change things in my diet, activities, and overall consumption. Without fail, I would feel better. I didn't understand that I was being guided by my higher self and was also completely guided by God and the Universe. Looking back, I now see experiencing countless disease as my training ground for my purpose to help others discover their own gifts in their own healing.

The More I Heal, the Stronger my Intuitive Gifts Become

During my young life, I started to note trends. My hands almost always burned when there was evidence of physical disease or injury. I could taste metal in my mouth around brain and blood disorders. And cancer always looked and behaved as irregular particles and shapes, while causing a flutter in my chest. I would share my experiences here and there, mostly at inopportune times like a dinner party hosted by my parents or with a store clerk.

My father wasn't around much, and when he was, he was never fully present. My mother was perpetually busy and overly concerned with others' perceptions. It wasn't until I became more vocal that I learned that what I lived daily was *not* commonplace. It made the abuse in my home worse and drove me further away from any feeling of belonging.

I longed to be a part of this system that rejected and dismissed me. So, I did what most children do to try to meet their needs. I hid in order to survive. I smeared whatever metaphorical mud I could over this part of me. There was a part of me that believed I never really existed. How could it be that the abuse I endured was being witnessed by so many in my life and that I actually mattered?

Despite feeling alone in my life, however, I had a knowing that I needed to continue forward.

Claiming My Gifts

When I was in my late forties, I was living alone for the first time in my life. I had been married twice, unmarried twice, and was recently recovering from the insidious effects of narcissistic and sociopathic abuse and CPTSD. I had eaten a whole lot of humble pie over the prior few years. Losing everything to gain myself was something I had accepted, although most people wouldn't understand it that way. I understood, and this was enough.

My small apartment was my safe haven. I called it my launch pad. The peace I found in this place and time was potent. Palpable. Even when I had to sit in my living room wearing my winter gear and gloves because the over 200-year-old house had a finicky furnace.

One of the greatest elixirs and medicines was that I was completely present. Completely safe. Completely surrendered to the healing work I had done and would do for myself and others. Nothing else mattered to me except my children and their lives. I hadn't realized how much I didn't have access to this peace and security until I experienced living on my own, without outside influences on any aspect of my life.

I meditated for four to six hours a day. I participated actively in healing, spiritual teachings, and travel. It was a great time of spiritual, physical, and quantum expansion. It was a place where I could move beyond the plateau I had reached over and over in my life. I was spiritually cleansed in ways I can't explain. Any and all disease became a memory of an experience I had had, rather than the state I had to endure every day.

I no longer looked over my shoulder in fear that my former husband would find me, or did so so much less, it was tolerable. I had learned to let go of the need to be needed; I didn't need much of anything in my life, with the exception of my health. Physical space and belongings meant nothing to me.

Nothing compared to this newfound coherence and alignment of my purpose and meaning—body, mind, spirit. For the first time in my life, I knew what it was to be free. I had no attachments to any person or thing, just openness to connection. I was finally free to express all aspects and dimensions of myself, to connect from one energy source with another.

This is a feat of epic proportions, when you are healing from a complete post-traumatic brain and nervous system.

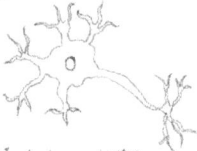

How TRAUMA AFFECTS THE BODY

NEUROLOGY:

Anxiety, depression, mood disorders, biochemical imbalances.

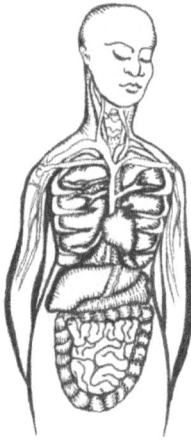

NERVOUS SYSTEM:

Imbalances in the nervous system cause other imbalances throughout the body.

TOXIN ELIMINATION:

Digestive problems such as constipation, IBS, gastritis, acid reflux, diarrhea, & inflammation.

IMMUNE SYSTEM:

Early childhood stress and trauma alters susceptibility to various diseases.

HORMONES:

Imbalances in sex hormones, like Estrogen, Progesterone, and Testosterone.

Unrepaired trauma can potentially affect any aspect and expression of the human physical body, energetic body, and spiritual body. Once the seed is planted, it chooses where to grow and surface.

I decided it was time I come out of hiding. Just as I opened my thoughts and interest to start somatic and healing work again, many of my former clients returned.

Others surfaced through happenstance, like meeting at a store or on a run, and even more came to me through referrals.

I was known for my ability to do deep healing work, to treat mystery illness, to see disease prior to diagnosis, and, for those who were open, to help change the trajectory of their entire lives toward what they felt called to do. The right people were guided to me. Without knowing me, they could tell there was something about me that could help them.

The conversation always went something like, "There's something different about you. I don't know what it is, but I think I need you to help me. What do you do? Can we set an appointment?"

I was regularly sought out by individuals from around the world, to help them heal from things they couldn't express with words. It was deeply driven from within their bodies, but the words rarely found form; rather they hovered on the tip of their tongue. I renamed my business Presque Vu 13. *Presque vu* means a so-called tip-of-the-tongue phenomenon. It is not really just a simple matter of forgetting something; instead, it is a strong feeling that you are on the very brink of a powerful epiphany, insight, or revelation, but it never happens. For example, you forget a name and you feel like you're about to say it, but you just cannot put your finger on it. That is why the *presque vu* phenomenon is associated with a feeling of incompleteness or near-completeness and just infuriating frustration.

It was a perfect description of our work together. I help remove the blocks causing incompleteness allowing the epiphany of one's true health and essence to shine through.

I helped find and heal the root cause of most mystery illnesses, including autoimmune diseases like fibromyalgia, Epstein Barr, and Lyme; anxiety, depression, and trauma, plus aided in recovery from addiction. As the days progressed, the list grew longer.

People often asked me how I do things, what my protocol is. Being that I am in flow and following a higher guidance, I never had a packaged answer, other than, "I just do it. It comes through me. The healthier I am, the more clear the channel." I think my reply frustrated people, because this wasn't a marketing slam dunk. There was no sales funnel or program to run someone through. I was just healing other healers in the most organic and original sense.

I knew that the way I healed was not necessarily the way others would heal. I also knew how it felt to "fail" trying to help someone, so I set out to become trained and certified in as many science-based, spiritual, or energetic disciplines and applications as possible.

As my voice grew strong, others surfaced whose voices were muted. They were ready to speak their own unique truth and share their gifts (or discover them). I understood this dynamic well. I was leaving a time of my own growth, where, metaphorically, I was exiting the woods after a long journey into its abyss.

I knew when it was time to enter. Without trepidation, I went under the canopy of hundred-year-old trees, just the moon, the stars, the sun, and me. A place in parts, where I was mute to myself, not understanding the depths of my own experience in my circumstances. The woods represented the container that I could unfold and become completely undone. Nature allowed me to empty without guilt or shame.

When I surfaced, I did so as more of me. Less of what I wasn't. The ease and clarity were palpable.

Fletch

At this time, I was introduced virtually to a highly regarded public figure, author, and successful military veteran named Fletch (name changed to protect his identity). Fletch retired as a fully decorated colonel and was a veteran of a recent war. He had since earned multiple master's degrees and done specialized training, plus created programs, facilities, and organizations to serve other veterans who had experienced trauma.

I was surprised how quickly we became friends. I mean, "Who am I? Just a girl who was coming out of the woods, having healed and shed much after an abusive and toxic marriage and traumatic childhood."

He reached out to me to ask my opinion about his program. He'd read that I served on mental health hospital advisory boards and liked "what I did." But something else was initiated when, in a phone call, he joked that he was as friendly as a wet dog.

I replied, "I usually steer clear of those types." Pausing and content, I breathed. "Seriously."

I was clear about who I let into my space. I don't care how much money, clout, or celebrity you have. I had learned how sacred our energy exchange is. I had also been married to an intelligence officer in the 5th Special

Forces. I know the unspoken trauma and its effects, when not addressed head-on.

I wondered out loud if his people-pleasing was a sign that he was activated. He didn't know it, but he had a knowing. He absolutely knew what I meant.

We hung up the phone, both pausing a minute before saying goodbye. I thought, *Do I say, "Talk to you soon?"* Or, *"It was nice knowing you, bye?"* It felt awkward, something I'm no stranger to.

He called back an hour later. His Southern accent thickened as he said, "Girl, I have never met anyone like you. You gave me pause, and I almost fell off my chair with how direct you are. Most people are intimidated by me. You just show up to be *with me*."

There it was. God's wink and the universe's nod came through in his next statement.

"I think you and I should talk. Really talk. I'm not sure with what, but I think you can help me."

I knew this wasn't our first time together. We had shared many lifetimes together. Souls recognize as souls.

"I am going to speak to you in my language," I said next. "You let me know how your energy responds."

He was rigid, structured, powerful, and had had an existential crisis. He had seen enough in his life to know that there is something special, and he embraced the esoteric. He said that he resonated with and was so interested to understand more. Something else we agreed on.

More by doing less.
Manufacturing less.
Thinking less.

Living in the state of the pause, knowing I would be guided to my next chapter, person, and stage of my journey.

No judgment, just truth. No people-pleasing or playing the networking game. Just one human to another, we agreed on an energy exchange and that we would walk this path together. He valued my insight and intuition. My authenticity was disarming and allowed him to leave his armor at the door. He let out an audible sigh and release.

Fletch was a gifted writer, prolific in his ability to bring the reader in close. His description of events from his traumatic childhood brought me to tears. Over time, he shared with me more of his unpublished stories, the ones that had no voice but followed him "like a bad smell."

His trauma most definitely began far before his twenty-eight years in the military. I told him this is what predisposed him to deeper wounding while in the military. I often asked him what the barrier was to being more authentic and sharing publicly, and he, being a gentleman, would politely change the subject.

Patience ~ I was Born with It

Fletch called weekly, and in between discussions of the projects we were working on, he started to confide many of his deepest and darkest experiences. He was a proud man who was regularly in front of the camera and on our TV screens. He felt safe within our friendship and healing relationship because of the standards we created.

I also had boundaries and sometimes walls. I was unaffected by his public persona and success. Most people wanted something from him and were trying to harm him or were intimidated by him. For better or worse, I was not like most people. I received the vision of why we were connected. I was being asked to serve.

We started to do some deeper trauma healing, and it was going well. He was making some significant positive changes and progress in his life when he reported to me that he felt free for the first time in his life.

"Girl, you are so refreshing I wish I could carry you around with me everywhere." He paused an honest pause. "Actually, I do. I hear your voice in my ear all the time."

We worked together and joined forces on a few more projects. Fourteen months flew by. Once, when we were together, he winced.

I looked at him and said, "That doesn't look good."

He confided he had a few minor health concerns and said he hadn't asked me to help, because we were already doing so much work.

"Health comes first," I replied. "Without it, you will not have sustainable success."

He agreed to have me do some in-person and remote psychic surgery. I did, and he felt relief. Then, he'd exhaust himself by overextending in other areas.

When I did remote work on him, I kept getting readings other than what he asked me to focus on. I didn't say anything to him, because he was going through a major business expansion and professional pivot. But it was hard to sit with.

"He has cancer," I confided with my therapist. She knew a little about him and a lot about me.

"Cancer. Are you sure?" She didn't love my connection with Fletch. But she loved my connection to the divine and my gifts. She was instrumental in my bringing them into light. She experienced it first-hand when she blurted out, "I want some of that good stuff! Tell me what you see with me... Don't hold back."

I was still shy about sharing. The root of my trauma went back lifetimes, of being persecuted for using my gifts. But I trusted her enough. "I've noticed from our first sessions together, your liver, kidney, and adrenals are shot. You have heavy-metal toxicity and brain trauma, mostly on your left side of your head. Something is going on in your left ear, and there I a negative spiritual entity in your thyroid." I took a deep breath. "There's more, but I think that's a good place to start." I suddenly didn't know where to place my arms and hands. Awkwardly, I crossed my them to keep them from flailing and then smiled, readying myself for the discard and dismissal.

Her eyes fixed on me—she is always dramatic and usually it has a positive effect, but this time our roles were flipped, and I thought, *Oh, I'm in trouble…* Though it will get smaller and smaller, there will always be a small part of me that is programmed to think something bad happens each time I show more of myself authentically. I know it will get better the more I practice presence and connection.

As the clock ticked, her mouth opened wide. I readied myself. Then she said, "You are spot on. I've been feeling really sick for months and trying to figure out what is wrong. Why the hell did you wait so long to tell me this?"

I shrugged my shoulders innocently, thinking, *Because you are my therapist…* But replied from another true position for me, "Because I didn't feel it is my place to say unless I'm asked. I've learned my lesson. It usually ends poorly. It's not spiritually ethical to go through someone else's energy without being asked to in some way."

Her laugh boomed around us, and she smiled her Mother-Earth smile at me. "Of course, I should have known. I've never met anyone like you, with this combination of gifts and integrity. I'm honored."

Knowing that it pained me to see this information in Fletch, and that it mattered to me that I handle it well because, well, I was exiting the woods and still fuzzy about all of the layers that existed between, she said, "Tell me what you saw with Fletchy. Are you *sure* it's cancer?"

I was sure. I had seen enough of it in my life that I knew how it presents.

"Yes, several types. In the blood, in his liver, and his prostate. Amongst other things. He's got spots on his lungs, his pancreas is about to give out, and he's got to know soon. Fuck. The human part of me is freaking out. My ego is screaming! This is too much."

She was close to falling off the rim of her seat in sheer disbelief at what I said, and maybe in awe. She leaned back in her chair and let out a sigh. "You have got to tell him."

I love her so much. She was always so present with me in all of my exploration and an important part of my homecoming. In the months following, she asked me to help her heal, as well, and my heart filled with even more love for her for how she trusted me.

Every time we worked together, I could see her own trauma releasing and letting go. She was further along on the journey than I was at the time, yet the residual effects of early childhood trauma and abuse take time to transmute for us all. This was the case for her. I respected her for her belief in healing and asking me to help. We both understood this and gave our multi-faceted relationship grace as we shared in this journey. We saw each other clearly.

Fletch, on the other hand, was in bad shape. I continued to get major hits from his pancreas, kidneys, now testes, prostate, and blood. I saw a vision of him passing out at a speech and vomiting bile.

My cell phone rang, and it was him. "I just had a bad spell. I don't even remember how I drove to the place, I was in so much pain. I ended the speech short and went around the building and passed out. I woke up and vomited. It was violent and disgusting." He made a joke, which I couldn't receive.

"No, stop. This is serious," I said, trying to talk some sense into him.

He said, "Girl, I wish you were here. I feel like I am surrounded."

I asked him if I could do some work on him. Before the words were out of my mouth, he yelled, "*Yes!*"

I told him I was going to work on his pancreas and set out for a run. I always did my best psychic surgery while running. I don't know if this is the way most do it, but for me, being outside, breathing in fresh air, increasing my energy, and going into a deep expression, increased my abilities.

The following month, I went on a trip to North Carolina, and Fletch came to visit. Though I didn't want say it, and I didn't want to know it, I could see, feel, taste, and smell how there was an intense conflict within his physical, spiritual, and emotional body. Dis-ease had turned into disease.

I thought, "It's better to ask if he wants to know." Consent is always key in a healing relationship, including consent to "see." In this case, I kind of was and kind of wasn't within consent. But I was guided to share.

We sat across from each other at a restaurant table. My eyes fixed on the candle as I exhaled deeply. "Listen. We have built this connection on authenticity and trust—."

Fletch interrupted. "I already know. I felt your energy in places of my body. My stomach pains have gone down by the way. No more vomiting bile, ha-ha! Seriously, girl, your energy is undeniable. Waiting to know has been killing me. I came all this way in part because you hadn't shared it with me over the phone. I thought you would, if I was in person. I want to know. So just tell me."

"First, I have to tell you that I believe you can heal any and all things. Anything that's in the physical can be healed in the spiritual and causal plane."

"Yes. If there is anything you have taught me, it's that. It's cancer, isn't it?"

"Yes. In the blood and in a few of your organs. We are going to be very structured about this. I have a plan. You have to get medical support, and we will do the rest together. Here's how we are going to heal it..."

Angela

I had just finished working with a beautiful couple who were going through IVF. They came to me on their last round of implantation and were worried. My primary client was Angela (name changed to preserve confidentiality), who thought they had lost their chance to conceive.

They had spent almost all of their savings, and she got a pull to reach out to me. I used to jokingly call my workspace "the last chance ranch," because, well, for many it was. I was their last chance or final hope. Esoteric healing and spirituality were in a strange place. It hadn't been commercialized and "whitewashed," yet. So, seeing a healer was not common practice.

Angela and I worked together for a few months, preparing her for implantation and fertility. In one guided healing, she was lying on a bed of earthy moss in the forest full of mother energy. Absolutely glowing. Before our work was complete, I saw her holding her baby in her arms. It was the universe's way of letting me know she was in alignment with this birth. How it would happen was not up to us.

Later, she messaged me, "I'm not pregnant. We lost our chance, and I'm not sure I can go through it again. Thank you for all of your help."

But in another timeline, I knew she was. I could feel the baby stirring, and I was bold enough to say so. How do I tell someone who has invested so much in a literal promise to understand that the desire result was coming? Just not in the way they planned.

"I know this is a heartbreaking time for you, but your baby is on its way. I can feel it. Have faith. I am here if you, need anything. I love you "

A few weeks later, she messaged, "We are pregnant! We are both in shock and scared and excited. It's so early on. But I wanted you to be one of the first to know. Thank you for all you have done for our family. We have learned so much about surrendering and working with universal energy, by living through this process. Words can't express how profoundly life-changing this experience has been."

Their son is beautiful, their destiny received.

Molly

Molly, a successful entrepreneur and "influencer," was abreast of Angela's entire journey and had watched it unfold. She reached out to me with a message that read, "I'd like to book a session. I think you can help me."

Molly had been without a period for over twelve years and had tried every program, doctor, protocol, and system to help her cycle again. She followed everything to a T. A literal perfect patient with less-than-optimal results.

As we started our work together, it was clear that her comfort zone was when she controlled the ball. This was completely understandable, especially with a woman who felt her body betrayed her for years, almost as much as medicine had. She had sought help and, time after time, had been unable to be guided toward a higher state of health.

A few sessions in, I felt the time was right to take some control and to guide. Smiling at her and sending love, I said, "Let's feel into the energy of a few things and timelines. Humor me."

She stopped and looked at me. Our eyes locked, and without a word, she nodded her head, Yes. We closed our eyes, and I brought her into a subconscious space where we could see and feel (her preferred intuitive sense).

We felt what healthy felt like to her, along with unhealthy, sad, free, flow, drive, etc. We bounced into different times memories in her life, and simultaneously, while I was guiding her, I felt into her body. As we shifted, it shifted from one energetic and physical imprint into another.

I could see where the conflict was and asked her a pointed question. "Keeping your eyes closed, what energy do you feel that is a constant throughout your life?"

Without skipping a beat, she whispered, "Restriction, measuring, and control." Then she said, "No flow."

Bingo.

I set her off with the homework to feel into all aspects of her daily life, work, and relationships, and to notice where there was restriction or control. She spoke to her live-in boyfriend and told him about her next point in our work together and her expansion. He brought a hammer up from the basement, put on some music, and handed it to her, gesturing to the food scale. She ceremoniously smashed every scale in their home. Food scales, body scales, anything that resembled a scale was smashed to smithereens.

The next week, she told me what she and her boyfriend did the night after our last session. I was ecstatic for them. "But why do you look sad?"

Molly said she felt blue and had noticed a huge pimple on her chin. "I never get pimples."

And I smiled. I could see her body returning to flow. She couldn't yet, but it was just a matter of time. Divine timing. At our next session, which was also the next full moon, Molly turned her camera on and was beaming from ear to ear. "I got my period!!"

I beamed back, shouting with my arms above my head, "You are in flow with the moon and your moon!"

Four years later, Molly still gets her period every month. Now, she helps guide other women to do the same.

Valeria

I was asked to help an adolescent by the name of Valeria (name and parts of the story altered, to maintain confidentiality).

I knew about Valeria through her mother and understood she was a fiery and determined young lady at the ripe age of twelve or thirteen.

One evening, I got the urge to text Valeria's mom (which is unusual) and thought, "Well, there must be a reason.'

Her mother immediately responded with, "Oh, Sharon, I am sitting in the back of the ambulance with Valeria. She fell and wasn't able to get up. She has lost all feeling from her waist down. I don't know what happened!"

I immediately asked if I could help in any way.

"Yes, please. But I don't know what you can do."

Via text, I asked permission to tap into Valeria's body and figure out what was going on. With consent, I continued and immediately felt pain in her lower back. I texted, "L4, 3, 2, and 1. Check there. I think there is a fracture. There is something in her atlas in the back of her neck where the skull meets the spine, pinched nerves and a small object."

A wave of nausea came over me. "Is she nauseous?"

"*YES!* She just said that she was."

"Okay, be careful not to strain her neck as you turn her, so she won't choke."

I continued to do a "diagnostic" and send via text. Later, her mother called.

"Sharon, I used your texts to tell the doctors what to look at. Everywhere you listed, they found something. I have no idea what you do, how you do it, or what you can do, but I trust you."

That became the way we ended our conversations, no matter how deep and challenging it might have gotten.

Valeria was later admitted to the hospital, paralyzed from the waist down. They had no conclusion as to how she became paralyzed. Everyone in the family was beside themselves. I had learned, if you have the capacity to help, you make sure you offer it without concern. I knew I could help Valeria, so I texted her mother, "I can help."

She said, "You have full rein."

We were in a global pandemic, so visiting a hospital was limited to emergencies and close family members only. Her mom set up a phone in front of Valeria, so we could use a video app.

Valeria looked at me with a distant look in her eye. I knew we needed time to connect without any influence from others, so I asked if everyone could leave the room for a bit, and they obliged.

Wasting no time, I was direct with her. "Hey, I know this is tough for you, but we are going to get you better, K?"

She muttered, "Okay."

"Hey, I am not going to hold back on anything, so if it is too much for you or if you don't understand, just ask!" I began to explain energy, our nervous systems, healing, and how we were going to approach her healing.

Valeria said, "It's weird. I haven't really talked with anyone about this kind of stuff, but it feels like I always have. I just wish I could get out of here. I want them to listen to me." It was then that I noticed her braces were off her teeth. "Yeah, Mom had them remove them, because they wouldn't do any scans to check my head where you told her to with them in my mouth."

I smiled and thought, *Well, how about that,* and allowed myself to absorb the full trust of this child, even though she was suffocating from the trauma (ancestral and otherwise) that she had yet to acknowledge and heal.

Then, we started our work with a distance healing. The thing that impressed me in our work together this first time was how open she was throughout the whole process.

"You are going to walk again. You are going to run again!" This became our mantra.

Her father, who thought I was her "meditation teacher," no matter how much she tried to explain it wasn't that, insisted I be a part of the team with the doctors who'd been assigned Valeria's care. She was released a week later in a wheelchair.

Her parents were advised that she needed to take care of herself on her own, so she learned to use her upper body to drag herself to the bathroom, down the stairs, and into her wheelchair. At our first in-person visit, her father had to lift her onto my treatment table. He hoisted her up, and she flopped down, face-first.

While she lay there, prone on her stomach, I helped her swing her legs onto the table to lie down. She and I made jokes about wherever we were blasting her off into another stratosphere that day in treatment.

Soon, I felt we had gotten our relationship to a level where I could go deeper into her emotional state. "I am wondering if you have experienced some trauma?" I asked. "Have you not felt protected and heard?"

It was then that Valeria and I were able to tap into the trauma she had experienced, and in turn unveil much of the generational trauma from both sides of her family line.

She was intensely brave, allowing us to go into any potential modality and subconscious state to get to the root of her pain, disease, and the figurative and literal paralysis.

A few weeks into our work, she looked at me and said, "I just want to walk again. I don't care how much pain I feel in my body, anything will be better than this."

We did several sessions of deep trauma healing and always ended with a visualization of her future self, doing something exciting. "I am going to be valedictorian of my class." Or, "I am a brain surgeon performing surgery."

And we would visualize and feel what it felt like to be doing what we knew she was determined and destined to do. We did somatic experiencing and soul retrieval, psychic surgery, and anything else I could to help clear the path and open up space in her spine to heal.

Already being aware we were close to this happening for her, I said, "By Sunday, you will be able to feel your toes, and if you continue this healing work, you will be walking and running again."

I spoke with her mother about deficiencies I had determined, and she immediately got the supplements at the store. Valeria attended physical therapy, and within a week was using a walker to lift herself up to standing. A week later, she was walking with a walker, and so on.

Her mother sent me video of Valeria pulling herself to stand and taking two steps by pulling her pant legs by herself to will her legs forward, saying, "Thank you!"

Valeria is now able to walk, run, and do extra-curricular activities. She continues her mission to be valedictorian, and when asked if I could share her story in this book, she replied, "If someone else can be helped by my story, I am all for it."

Jose Carlo

Once again, the universe introduced me to a beautiful soul, whom I later was asked to help with energy and healing work. She herself was a healer and had heritage in Colombia.

She was a trained healer and had a beautiful and dynamic family. We had a few sessions and were scheduled for a follow-up when I received a text.

"Sharon, I need your help, my son, Jose Carlo, is in the hospital in California and was admitted for a potential brain issue."

I asked permission to go into his physical body and perform an assessment, which determined he was having a stroke. In addition, I noticed a bleed and informed her of the same. He was in critical condition. I worked for over twenty-four hours on Jose Carlo and continued to stay in touch with his mother via text. She went to the hospital in California to be with him in the ICU.

Jose received excellent medical intervention and in addition was under full care by his angels and my psychic surgery team. His mom later told me that his bleed was discovered after my text, and it stopped very quickly. After some weeks, Jose was released to his mother and flown home to rehabilitate. I was then called to come to the house and work directly on him.

I, of course, was excited to meet Jose n person and start our continued work and assessments. He was very weak and had a peg port still in his stomach. He was still experiencing paralysis to the point he had trouble swallowing. His walk was limited, and he tired easily.

When I walked into his room, he smiled from ear to ear and said, "I feel like I know you."

I smiled. Many times, the recipient of healing experiences the energetic fingerprint and essence of the healer. I said, "We have met in another realm." He tilted his head and nodded, showing his understanding.

I asked Jose what his goals were, and he replied, "To go back to school." According to his mother, this was a tall order, if not impossible.

I looked at Jose and checked in with his guides. "Let's give it all we can, shall we?"

We worked together every week. Very quickly, Jose gained strength. One by one, the aids to walk, eat, swallow, etc., were removed. His mother told me, a few weeks in, he refused to work with any of his care team and would only attend my sessions. Everything else, he blatantly refused.

I laughed and said, "Well, it looks like we are doing okay for now, but let's encourage him to go to his doctor checkups to measure his success."

Each week, his progress was astounding. He told me that he was getting bored, so he and his brothers went for a drive and found an old motherboard for a computer system. He took it home and tried to make it into a 3-D printer. I thought that was a lofty goal, considering the significant amount of brain trauma he was healing.

Jose was a sweet and determined young adult. We always took fifteen minutes before we commenced the healing to discuss whatever was on his mind. He opened up significantly, and we both looked forward to the week's topic. One week in particular, he greeted me with his usual grin and said, "Wait here!"

Within a minute, he returned with a palm-sized orange plastic elephant. Each limb moved, and the trunk faced upward. I thought, "How cute."

Jose asked, "Do you know where that came from?" When I shook my head no, he added, "The 3-D printer I made from scratch."

Beaming with joy and gratitude, I fought back the lump that was responsible for my choked words. "You are incredible! This is incredible!"

As I handed it back to him, he put up his hand. "No, I made it for you." In that moment, I realized I tangibly held one of the most intangible gifts that had ribboned its way into my life. Evidence of the Universal law of cause and effect. My saying *yes* to my healing had opened space for Jose, and so on.

Jose continued our healing sessions and continued his progress. Working, going to local college, and ultimately, you guessed it, he went back to his college in California to complete his final undergrad semester.

Chapter Six

The Fire Starter

The crunch under our feet as we walked reminded us that we were in the thick of autumn. A few grounded leaves were caught by the gust of wind created by a passing car. I watched them dance in a synchronized upward spiral.

I heard, "Autumn leaves have a palpable knowing." I had that knowing, too. Most of my life, I had expended energy to hide and extinguish it, with my greatest expression tied to my greatest pain. Whispers from a voice I call the wise one who knows. They always provide me with strength, when I think I have none. The wise one who knows always carries me through.

I laughed to myself, thinking about my life. From one bump to another, I had surrendered—or so I thought—to a life as a healer.

No matter how much I abandoned myself, the infrequently practiced language of my own special knowings never left me completely. I wanted to fit in. I wanted to feel connected, loved, and supported by family, friends, and colleagues. So, I worked hard to cover the things I thought made me different, hard to relate to, and invisible. In many ways, I was born invisible, destined to go unseen in the world of a family and parents who had a hard time seeing anything, while they fixated upon their gaping wounds.

Whatever language I spoke in the womb was my native tongue. It wasn't the first time it had been spoken, but it was the language I first learned lifetimes ago. I'm not sure if I knew it then, but I know now it is the way I communicate with the universe.

Even when I thought I wasn't.

Looking back, my soul spoke in countless ways without ever requiring words. I learned it is even better when you find another who can openly do the same. Many of my clients and patients do. My children do. Complete strangers do. But not the rest of my family.

I wish this was our primary form of communication. This knowing, planted within. The eternal existence of the soul housed in a physical body has infinite ways of communicating and connecting, but always through the vehicle of our soul and mind. All souls are firmly positioned in the physical heart. And in the metaphysical. It was always where I'd run from or to, when times were tough. No matter how much I tried to manipulate the truth, it stood strong, the place to hold any conflict and not break. It whispered to me in a kaleidoscope of ways every day, saying, "Set me free."

As a child, I'd sit on the railroad-tie wall in my backyard, my feet dangling like a ball at the end of a chain. I'd see glimpses of this day and beyond. My hands would bloom like snowflakes as they reached out to people across the globe, healing the unseen. Tending the liberation of their souls, as I liberated mine, too. Year after year, I was shown this vision over and over in a variety of ways. But had I shown what I had to go through along the way, I'm not sure I would have joined the journey.

There is something to be said about not knowing the details of what lies ahead. Fear always requires information. Faith carries you forward with a knowing, into a deeper knowing. To not know anything. I realize now I always leaned into my highest self. It is a level of oblivion, wildness, and pure absolution to the divine truth.

"Each day, we are born anew." I heard these words frequently, and on the days when I didn't hear them, I still chose to find ways to become renewed. To empty and reinvent, until I got the feeling in my gut, like a train coming to its home station. It knows its tracks are at the end, but this set point unfolds to its new journey. I would seek this like a journeywoman traveling the world for treasures. The greatest ones I found were the pieces of my soul I had yet to meet.

It wasn't every day that I chose to lean into the obscure. I toggled between two worlds from birth. To know your purpose at the age of eight is a gift. To share it with others and then be abandoned, dismissed, abused, and rejected at such a young age is indescribable, painful, and isolating. Now I know it was this very experience that gave me the metaphysical muscle to get through this next season of coming undone. My strength and determination that came from understanding that my health, good, joy, and calling were on the other side of my efforts got me through every storm I had to survive throughout my life.

Activation

Like summer coats us with its warmth and protection from the cold, hushing the harsh bite of winter, autumn brings a crisp clarity to our senses. It asks us to awaken, allowing us to prepare for the next season.

This autumn's magnification was different altogether. It was silenced by the energetic and ominous tension that was my second husband, Andy.

It didn't begin this way. I was divorced from my first husband and now remarried. I thought, this time, I had chosen love. I felt an indescribable "chemistry": part passion, part being needed and desired. He communicated from a place that felt like home. My home. Everything else about our lives didn't matter. We "knew" that our connection was meant to be.

A priest who had known Andy since he was a child described him best: he had a humble charm that, when he left your presence, made your heart stir and ache, even just a little. For me, it ached a ton. I couldn't figure out why.

I later learned that, hidden under his humility, there was a darkness that defied gravity. At its worst, it was a Category 5 hurricane living in a bottomless abyss. In my darkest of days and confusion after I left Andy, I called Father Ron, who invited me to his home. I was a shell of my former self in all ways. I felt traumatized, afraid, alone, and determined never to be in this place again.

I sat with Father Ron for a few hours. Perched on the edge of his sofa, my arms leaning on my knees and my hands holding my head, I spoke about my confusion, questioning my life, love, and how this happened.

SHARON LAND

"How could his family not tell me how bad he was? How could our friends not say anything?" It was something I didn't understand and had lived through my entire life. My karma. "Lack of context and protection."

Even as I sit writing this at the foot of the Garden of the Gods Park in Colorado, I try not to judge myself. So, if you are, I don't blame you. I had found a home in the mouth of a fire-breathing dragon. I would be lying if I didn't mention that there was a thrill coupled with the fire that I had to walk through to find his heart. His love could rarely be found, except for his mother.

Revisiting this relationship years later brings up to me the hologram of the two timelines I experienced simultaneously: an undying love and commitment with the one I thought I had survived everything else in my life to find, someone so rare; and one who existed parallel to the biggest nightmare of my life, where I was almost killed many times over. I was healing and letting go of both.

Smoke burned my nose. Father Ron had a tracheotomy and would hold it closed to suck back the smoke of his cigarette. As he spoke, smoke expelled from his orifices like a dragon. After each inhale, father exhaled channeled words and messages of the divine. Rhythmically, he'd take a breath in and his eyes would roll back, while mine became wider, flitting back and forth from the ashtray to his face. Our connection was the metronome keeping time to the anticipated exhale, a recount of Andy's spiritual journey and his wounded soul. The exchange of smoke, rhythm, purging, and synchronicity became the pacing of the energetic in and out.

Intuitively, I knew part of Father's epiphany was how his aura expressed his own bittersweet heartache that had manifested in his own physical disease. Under calloused skin, his soul sang the song of conflicted acceptance. His own journey was bittersweet and broken, much like that of the souls he yearned to serve.

This is from beyond, I thought. I tried to hide the burning as I squinted tears from my irritated eyes. The smoke was painful, while the words were a salve to my soul. *Here we go with the dichotomy*, I thought, as I recognized the familiar pattern. Space held for me was consistently accompanied by pain that I was ashamed to admit, even if it was being caused by the person in front of me.

Father Ron's energy reminded me so much of Padre Pio's, my patron saint, the wounded healer. You would not have known he was a priest or healer, either. Father was rough in most ways, his voice brash, his energy thick, as he lived a life of ambiguity and dual existence, but always in service to God. It was Andy who introduced me to Father Ron and to Padre Pio, his progeny and, most important, my patron saint. One was in the spirit, the other in the flesh. Right here, right now.

Father channeled during much of our time together. His full-bodied space, created by his wisdom as God's instrument, narrowed to an awkward, standing human who limped to the door and waved goodbye to me. His service to me was overruled by his allegiance to the family I just left. Ego became the punctuation of our exchange. He was doing God's work, but he, too, was just as human as any of us. He chose allegiance to the many instead of one.

Was it because I was a seemingly broken version of me? Or did he already know the happy ending?

The first time Andy called me beautiful, he pronounced it the same way my Granny Marie did. "Bee-uuuu-teee-full." He was seemingly generous in his attention and went out of his way to tell others how much he loved me.

I spoke with my then friend Alyssa, telling her that things didn't add up. I just felt something was off. She told me that she'd never seen anyone so in love the way he was. She gave me examples and told me I'd be a fool to end it. I knew I had avoidant tendencies and thought, "Here you go, ruining from something because you're scared." I often talked myself out of my intuition, because I had no concrete evidence to my sense.

I had to learn:

"Your intuition rarely makes sense to you in the moment. Follow it anyway."

Many times, Andy sat on the edge of the bed, hovering over me while I slept. He would brush back my hair and tearfully whisper, "You are an angel sent from heaven for me and V. You are the reason I had to come back. To come and find you. To love you .

I have two daughters whom I love and who are my world. Simultaneously, I had never felt so needed and loved as I did with him. I touched his cheek and felt so gratefully in love.

He brought a combination of protection and effusive love into my world. I overlooked the chaos and confusion he caused day after day, choosing to surrender to him. I consciously unlocked and opened every door to my universe, though he never came close to the threshold of many of them.

"You aren't that loveable. Not everything about you is good or perfect. See? Even he says so."

The energy of waiting was comfortable and familiar to me. So, I stayed in the queue.

He was the father of an adorable little girl and a survivor of a near-death experience, an NDE. He had suffered TBI and PTSD from an accident where he had died and was revived at least four times.

I remember my mother telling me about it years prior, as she gossiped about what her friend/his Aunt Theresa had told her. "A friend of yours from high school is in critical condition at the hospital. They don't think he's going to make it. My friend is beside herself." When I asked his name, she couldn't recall. Her information superhighway always ended abruptly.

I realized the connection between my calling and TBI, PTSD, and neurological disorders caused by trauma. My first husband, Tom, suffered several brain injuries as a student athlete and, later, in the Fifth Special Forces Unit, where he served for six years. I still didn't understand the depths to which this would take me, until I was divorced after twenty-three years and became involved with Andy.

Years later, when Andy and I spoke for the first time, I learned it was him who my mom had been talking about. I hung up the phone after a two-hour call and connected the dots. My heart did a jump. "Holy shit, it was him! Well, I'm happy he's alive. I'm happy we got to connect."

Then sadness hit me in waves. My heart broke. I wished I could have been there for him back then. It seemed so silly of me to feel this way, but I did. And I told him so the next time we spoke.

After our first call, I felt the crackling energy of big change ahead. After the second, it hit. Big, *big* change was coming.

His accident was serious. He had been t-boned by a truck going 30 miles per hour while he was riding his Harley. A bunch of kids were flying to the liquor store. The crash flung him thirty feet in the air, hard enough to toss his helmet over and get caught in the telephone and electrical wires lining the street. He was thought to be dead on arrival.

Our high school friend, Brett, was the first officer on the scene. Later, in a message to me, Brett said, at first, he didn't know it was Andy. He said his skull had been split wide open and the femoral artery in his leg was severed. He was bleeding out and assumed DOA. Brett told Andy the same account. Normally a stoic guy, Brett vomited at the scene, when he made the connection that this lifeless body was his longtime friend.

Andy died and was revived in the hospital at least four times. Eventually, he was put in a medically induced coma for six weeks. He later shared with me his vivid memories of his time crossing over. On his darkest days, which became more and more frequent, he always said he wished he'd died. He told me his grandmother met him at the gate to cross over, and she told him he wasn't finished yet. That he had to go back. At first, he said he thought it was for V. Later, he said it was because he had to meet and marry me.

Years later, he claimed to know that he had met his wife during the first conversation we had on the phone.

His daughter informed me this same thing only the second time I was with her, on the cusp of her seventh birthday. She immediately took to me and called me Mom, which I thought was strange, but attributed it to her being abandoned by her biological mother. I didn't mind and had plenty of love in my heart to give. It wasn't uncommon for people to connect with me this way. Most of my training clients became part of my extended family, and many called me Mom.

On V's birthday, I went to their house. I got on the floor and played with her, helping her build jumps for the Breyer horses I had bought for her seventh birthday. She placed her tiny hand on mine to feel the movements I was making, as she studied me, listening to my energy as much as to my voice. There was something kindred and familial about us together. I ignored when she spastically elbowed me while trying to mimic the motions I showed her. I knew the energetic imprinting that was happening.

As we named all of the horses she now proudly owned, V toggled her focus from me to the horses. I felt like someone visiting a baby monkey. I had entered her world, and she was fascinated. Her tiny hand explored my hair, face, and jewelry. She kept repeating that I was so beautiful, and she wanted to look just like me. Part feral, part princess, she expressed so much through motion. One second, she was on the floor, and the next second, on my lap, staring me squarely in my eyes and touching my lashes. I studied her, too, noting the pinned bangs she had cut back with safety scissors, adding over twenty clips to frame her face. The Hello, Kitty and heart shapes added to her expression. Patiently, I let her explore, knowing this was all new to her.

Her name was Genevieve. I thought, *What a beautiful name*, very similar in feel and era as my daughters', Emily and Elizabeth. V was taller than an average kindergartner, with a tiny body that could almost fit into a doll's clothes. Her smile took up more than half of her face. Most of her front teeth were missing, and she was covered with chocolate all of the time.

On our second or third time together, giddy with excitement, V scaled over several couches and jumped onto a chair to greet me. She yelled to her father like he was in the next county, as he walked up the stairs behind me. "Dad, can I tell her? Can I, Dad? You know, the *secret!*"

Pausing to smile at us both, he continued walking. When Andy smiled, his eyes lit up, the lines surrounding them accentuating the feeling. I heard him laugh and say, "Bull in a china shop," as he walked down the hall.

In a louder and more excited tone, she said, "Well, can I?"

I had just come into the house and attempted to lower the bags of food I'd brought. She stood on a chair, attempting to meet my eyes as she cupped my face with her little sticky hands. Flashing a chocolate smile, she blurted out the next words with a chunk of Oreo cookie visible through her big teeth. As I was thinking, *Does this kid have any rules?* she spluttered, "My dad's going to marry you."

I froze, until the violent, ripping crunch of my paper shopping bags brought me back to focus. The truth is, I thought about Andy all the time, stunned by the uncanny connection we had on every level in our conversations. It was as though he knew my soul. Something in my body did a flip-flop, thinking about a commitment. My divorce wasn't final from my first marriage. I had been on a healing journey for over fifteen years.

There was something I couldn't put my finger on with this connection. I remembered a session with a shaman who talked about control. He said that our greatest moments came from the presence of our experiences, not the controlling of them. When he spoke the words I was saying then in my head, I knew this wisdom. It was deeply ingrained within me.

I wanted to run. I always wanted to run, when it came to commitment. Someone I was dating asked me which side of the bed I preferred to sleep on, and without skipping a beat, I replied, "The side closest to the door."

But I no longer wanted to run. I just didn't know how to stay. I decided my way of trying to control the outcome would not win today. So, I stayed. I stood still while my inner world was on fire. I thought I was growing. I smiled at V and tried to trust that this was meant to be.

When your choices come from a lack of trust in self, you are not accessing your intuition. You are confirming your fears.

We quickly moved in together, in part because of the need for me to have all three girls under one roof. But there was another part that was driving this fast commitment: I had a fear that the distance would change how he felt about me. The move to my house meant I was first driving my girls to school and then V an hour to hers. Then, I drove back to the barn to prepare for training fourteen horses and lessons. Afterward, I would pick up the girls and bring them all to the barn to finish the evening. It was a big commitment on my end, but having my own business as a trainer afforded me the luxury of creating room in my schedule to take on more responsibilities.

Andy needed to rest. He'd been on a six-year-long survival, or so I thought. I gave him grace, while I took on the additional responsibilities. That was what we were supposed to do, right?

Instead of bringing home a puppy, I brought home V. My daughters looked at me like I had fully lost it when they came home to find a feral seven-year-old jumping off the back of our sofa.

Barely speaking coherently through my guilty smile, which I tried to contain, I mouthed, "What?" in response to their shocked faces. Their eyes opened wide and their mouths were agape as they pointed to the dogs, who were scooting and running for cover. I could almost see word bubbles above their heads, asking, "What is *this*?"

I smiled and gently waved to Emily and Lizzy to sit. V needed some modeling and mentoring. I intuitively hoped their behavior would help to evolve this little monkey princess jumping bean. I had been programmed to believe this was my job. And Andy confirmed this through his constant exhaustion and exasperation with being a single father.

"She needs a mother and a woman to show her how to be a lady." That was all I needed to hear. Co-dependency says we are responsible for others' pain. I never wanted anyone to experience the pain I had in my life. I had a tremendous capacity for suffering, survival, and pain. I made it look easy. This was not the thing I wanted to become famous for, but it was true in this moment.

Breaking the ice, I blurted out, "Who's hungry?"

Hearing only V answer, "*Me!*," I went into the kitchen to make a batch of homemade nachos. I heard both of my girls cackling in disbelief.

At fifteen, Emily was amused by how fiery and boundless little Genevieve was. In her usual way, she took under her wing those people and animals who had been discarded. She had a staying force within her for those who were the most challenging to deal with. Lizzy, at nine, was not amused at the least. I noticed her tics slowly return. My response was, "It will get better "

I prayed for V. For all of us. We were living in a home that, at any moment, could be padlocked shut by the bank. My first husband had left me with a ton of debt plus a bunch of shutoff notices and a mortgage that had been unpaid for over a year. I had no idea what would come next. I just took it one day at a time. Any time I felt I was white-knuckling my life, I'd let my hands open and say, "I'm open to receive."

When they first moved in, Andy slept in my girls' room, and they bunked with me. Each night, I was flanked by Lizzy and V in my king-size bed. Emily moved into a bedroom we converted for her in the basement. She was usually happy to have some distance between herself and her sister.

V watched everything Lizzy did and tried to imitate it. Lizzy would hug me and play with my hair, so V, too, would fight to do the same. Lizzy wouldn't move, so V would shove. Lizzy would resist, and they'd use me like a doll. I became a tug of war toy between them, my hair pulled, body squashed, and spirit tired.

Most times, I felt like I needed a break from being *on* all of the time. I'd lie in bed between them, waiting for them to drift off to sleep, so I could peel them off of me. Sometimes, I'd sleep on the floor, because I needed the energetic space. I just wanted them to be at peace, so I could feel some of my own.

I sought peace any way I could, even though it might be misguided.

One of my favorite and most peaceful moments with Andy was when he'd pray the rosary. I'd find him on the bed at different times of the day, and I'd lie down beside him as he whispered the Our Father and Hail Mary over and over. The breathing, whispering, and clink of the beads as he rearranged them on his chest recreated the sacred sound of my shaman. With one hand on his heart and the other on his sternum, I'd quietly recite with him while simultaneously praying for his own healing.

I sheepishly shared that I was a healer and could help him with much of his pain. We bonded over the work I did on him. Body. Mind. Spirit. I could hear the silent and tortured screams of the unmetabolized emotional and physical pain that was stored inside his body. I saw his foot crushed to pieces and tasted the metallic rods holding his hips together.

The work I did was some of my proudest to date. I had come a long way in my own healing and was openly working with a few clients as a medical medium, metaphysician, and somatic healer. His was the most extreme in all ways. The peace on his face after our sessions made me happy. I felt good, being of service to the one I loved. I needed him to need me.

As days strung along, I felt as though I was following a never-ending path, seeking the future projections he'd cast. "If I can just…, then I will be able to do…"

The work mostly fell on my shoulders. His words said exactly what I needed to hear, but his actions were completely contrary. I continued to be confused. Our faith connected us, but his extreme anger and magnified reaction to little things became more and more bizarre. I thought he needed more support. When I communicated my concerns, he asked for my patience.

He was speaking right into my programming:

I was born with patience. *"I dieted for your entire pregnancy…"*

I was born without needing much. *"You were such a good baby, you just lay in the playpen, ate, and slept."*

I was programmed to find my worth inside someone else's eyes. *"Your mother loves your sister more than you."*

I was good at creating temporary happiness by taking responsibility for other people's pain.

I know how tremendously strong I am.

I had already recovered from a stroke and bounced back better than before. I was still healing from this, mostly on my own through protocols, which I had intuited for myself.

There was something within me that knew Andy was my greatest challenge yet. The most wounded and distantly dark. His inconsistent pull in and push away was normal to me.

I knew my calling was in healing. I had already created a small following of fellow healers whom I had helped to heal things that doctors were baffled by. I thought God was testing me, and I was determined to pass the test. I always wanted to pass any test with flying colors.

I somehow confused needing to prove my abilities through a relationship with my partner.

So, as I added more onto my list of responsibilities, Andy grew more indignant, so I would try harder. The more I communicated how much I was trying, how I needed his help, the more he would tell me I was much better at this than he was. He would romanticize stories of his "glory days," which were comprised of his ambling through the country, "living."

He left college in the last semester of his senior year to take off to parts unknown. Arizona, Montana, California, where he immersed himself in nature while exploring and living a hedonistic life. He smoked weed like cigarettes, did lots of drugs, including psychedelics and whatever he could get his hands on. His eyes sparkled when he spoke of the parties he attended and the women he was with. He always seemed to be the hero or victim of circumstance. Occasionally, when it suited him, he acknowledged being the villain of many exchanges with women.

He would say that our mutual friends (all married now) had secretly told him they envied him for following his dreams and living that way. Traveling, writing, exploring, and adventuring—living a hedonistic life.

The reality of our lives in the present felt so different than the promises he made when we first dated. The more I took on, the further away from the promises he got. The more I asked him about our agreements, the more effort he made to be out of the house.

In stark contrast to where we had started, I began to find him drinking and smoking weed with our neighbors, while I was helping the girls with their homework, cooking dinner, driving to voice lessons, teaching lessons, etc. It felt like betrayal. It never failed to create an ache deep in my chest, each time I heard him retell the stories of his past. I was exhausted and felt cheated that he'd drive right past my barn, knowing I had his daughter with me.

V went from sweet to unruly. She was disruptive and oppositional. At times, she was even dangerous because of her ignorance about barn and horse safety and her refusal to listen to anyone. One by one, my clients tried to help, but returned to me with the same look in their eye. The same look riders have after they are systematically bucked off the same horse. Each one of them would go sailing over her left shoulder after a quick duck, right torso twist, lean backward, and thrust forward. I knew it well, as I was the one who had to rehab her from this disposition. Each one landed flat on their back, staring at the sky, saying, "What the f* just happened?" The look of anger, hurt, terror and "out of my league." Each person who helped would return V-less. they weren't down for the ride.

Our whole house was uprooted by this little forty-pound seven-year-old. And by her father, who slowly but surely removed himself from any parenting responsibilities.

When I got home after a long day, with kids in tow, I'd find him half drunk, telling his stories. They were repetitious. At first, I ignored them. Later, I attempted to redirect the conversation. But he would continue on making statements about how I was jealous, lazy, or insecure. He had no problem publicly humiliating me.

He would finish his repertoire for his audience by stating he had, "died unto himself. Been touched by God twice, after returning home from the rehabilitation facility," where he'd learned to walk again, and was returning to life the best he could. That he was a wretched, broken man now, "carrying his cross."

Wait! Did he think *I* was I his cross? That was a far cry from what he called me in the beginning.

He left us all speechless. And me, I was energetically paralyzed and utterly confused. I was short-circuiting from the lack of presence in my reality. Others were in rapt attention, because they loved a good story of rebellion and debauchery.

I could tell, on this particular autumn day, things were going to be rough on our walk. He was chain smoking, after being up all night getting high, and was stone cold.

We left the girls in the house. V wanted to join us but was gruffly told no, so she stormed back into the house and slammed the door behind her. This had become commonplace, as she was acting out more now that she was feeling more comfortable. Her reaction took his festering anger into a full boil.

As we walked, I could hear him suck on his cigarette and "*poooooof*" out the smoke. In between, he mumbled, No-good fucking psycho," "God, send your son. Please come and finish this once and for all," "Separate the wheat from the chaff and remove the sinners."

I had never understood this part of Biblical teachings and accepted this as his belief.

He was holding the leash of our dog, sucking the air out of the leash's fabric like he was of all of us. He acknowledged me in expletives, as if I wasn't there.

I whispered the words, "It's okay." His fury was mounting and, somehow, the arrow of anger at things that happened "to him" that day was turning decidedly toward me. Somehow, I felt strong. Somehow, I felt calm as his storming grew. Of course, looking back now, there was nothing to be calm about as I stepped one more foot toward and into his darkness.

I stood still and quiet, trying to reach the wounded part of him. I was reaching into him as a psychic surgeon, trying to disarm this explosive, my energy mirroring a highly trained bomb squad leader's. I was quiet, practiced at the job, highly skilled, and deeply aware of the potential explosion with one wrong move.

I moved slowly toward the evidence of the wounded soul of a seven-year-old boy. I could see him clearly, since he came to visit me frequently. The boy who was imprisoned by the thorns of his trauma and his past. The boy who shared stories of a man who would come into his room in the dark and do unspeakable things to him. Who shared stories of drinking at age nine and not stopping until he flipped his car over on a highway in Arizona.

The more we walked, the further I felt myself entering the dragon's den. This dragon was angry. He was hungry for blood.

We walked down a path that led to a cornfield. We lived across from a farm that grew and sold corn to local stores and had a corn maze shaped into the rows. It was late in the season, and the stalks had now dried and been cut down, leaving acres and acres of chopped-up dry stalks.

He let my dog Cooper off the leash and threw a stick. Cooper had the body and front legs of a basset hound, the head of a Jack Russell, the back legs of a beagle, and a heart of pure gold. I got Cooper when Elizabeth was a toddler and Emily was in grade school. Their faces lit up with delight when I picked Emily up from the bus with our new puppy. Always happy, silly, and loving, Cooper was the glue that held us together when we were all clearly falling apart. Especially during my divorce. Now, years later, he still pastored us all.

Andy was standing on the edge of a path next to the corn, his head covered by the hood of his sweatshirt. For the first time, he was looking directly at me. But his eyes were looking right through me. I could see he wasn't there, though. That he was in a place where he was the recipient as well as the aggressor of a dark, spiritual torture. Telepathically, I could hear the voices in his head. I could see his spirits sparring, a war unto himself. The duality and dichotomy of a tortured man. It was as clear as day right in front of me. With the face of an angel, Andy could disarm you with a glance. But his demons were out for blood, and in this moment, they were winning the fight.

I could hear my heart beating in my ears. My chest was hot, and my hands were tingling still from trying to reach into him. Silty darkness seethed from his body like billowing smoke. It didn't look like him anymore, and I felt the urge to run. As he stared right at me, he sucked so hard on his cigarette that his right eye involuntarily squinted, and he started to choke and cough.

As he smacked the pack of Marlborough Reds on his palm, the clack-clack-clack echoed around us. Still staring, he slipped another cigarette out of the pack, flicked his butane lighter open, and struck the gears to light the flame. It came out unbelievably high and created a black soot stain on the cigarette that hung from his mouth.

Flicking his embers and first cigarette into the dried crushed corn, he looked me up and down.

I said, "Hey, don't do that. This whole field will catch in a second!" I went to find the embers in the corn.

Andy pulled a crumpled piece of colored paper from his pocket and lit it then held that to a dry stalk, lighting it on fire. He was still staring. But now, he was smiling.

I watched the flame catch hold and couldn't believe what I was seeing. "What are you doing?! We've got to put this out!" The fire swiftly grew, with the wind aiding its travel.

It was then that I completely left my body. From a vantage point near the clouds, I saw myself walk away from the fire. I don't know how Cooper made it home. I don't know how I did, either. I vaguely recall standing on my deck, watching the smoke billow from the field. Fire truck sirens screamed, and I faded into darkness.

I found myself again in that cave. Naked, cold, and alone. Somehow, the familiarity was comforting.

The darkness was broken by a flicker of light. I found myself in my room, lighting a candle with the face of Mary on the front.

Staring at the flame was all I could do.

Chapter Seven

The Drive To Go Home

And know this, my heartfelt breath, the heaviest, most profound, penetrating touch you bestow upon me is when in mind, body, and transcendent spirit ... we are one in unconditional Love.

The vast sea in which we swim has many mountains, valleys, and caves amongst which I burned to swim freely. Then again, we met after traversing many paths... Now, I fight the good, true fight to stay in your wake and grow closer by your side. Please patiently wait 'til I know how to perfectly fulfill your every desire"
Signed,
Your husband

I was in my forties and still had never experienced what home felt like. I searched, I traveled, I slept with, I restricted, I let go, I medicated, I paid big bucks to attend personal growth seminars, I bought the books and still, somehow, I had denied myself of home in all ways. I bought and paid for things I thought would bring it to me. But I never found it.

I realized, and maybe you do now, too, I was stuck with the sense that I never truly knew what it felt like to be at peace and safe within myself or any container. Not at a family home, school, or friend's house. Not in body, brain, or energy. Neither internally or externally.

This is the reality of being raised in a chaotic environment where my least stressful moments were achieved because I learned to have few to no needs. I had no fight left after the constant pressure to perform to satisfy someone else's unmet, unfulfilled black hole of needs. I hope you read that again and see where you might be *exerting your energy training for someone else's fight.*

This was so natural for me. Definitely not healthy, though... July 19 marked the day that I, rather than run away from something, ran toward a place I now call home.

Myself.

"The opportunity to pivot isn't always brought on by you, but when it comes, grab it with both hands and get ready for the ride of your life. To save your life. To change the trajectory of your life."

July 19 was another pivot point. My biggest one to date.

Andy was standing at the dresser in our bedroom, facing the television, while I was on the bed. He wasn't watching TV; rather, he was using it as a place to fix his eyes. He was in the midst of another psychotic break.

These came frequently once we moved to Florida, and in fierce waves. I thought back to the month before we reconnected. I was in complete shock because of what I had experienced and become. I had spent years, *decades* unbecoming what wasn't in alignment with who I was.

But these past few years had landed me back in an unhealthy space. Unfortunately, I blocked out anyone who tried to tell me this. I didn't and couldn't hear anything from anyone. I had put everything into this marriage because of its promise and my illusions.

For my entire life, I had worked hard to make a home and a hearth. But now, in this moment, I felt the furthest from home I ever had. I was living my worst nightmare. Isolated from my family, friends, and my business I had grown from nothing, I was alone on an island, surrounded by hungry sharks.

I'd wake in the middle of the night in a panic to see the covers pulled back, revealing the empty spot he'd occupied in our bed, and never knowing how or where I would find him next. Would he be dead or alive? Drunk or stoned? Receptive or Deceptive? I realize now he was all of these at once, but my brain only let me see what it was ready to see.

My biggest concern was I didn't want our children to be the first to find him. Visions he had planted in my head included his brain being splattered on the wall behind the couch in the garage. I lived in a constant state of panic, hypervigilance, and chaos. I was fighting to survive. I was fighting to protect the kids. I was fighting for his healing. And I was failing us all miserably.

Out of fear, I hid the gun he bought just prior to our move to Florida. On the days when his darkness was especially bad, I'd rush home, praying he had left it at the house. It didn't matter how many times I had to do it, I was always energetically repulsed to touch it. Even though my first husband, Tom, was a police officer, I always felt uneasy around guns. So, I used a washcloth to wrap it, pick it up, and put it in my suitcase, which I tucked away in my closet.

It wasn't hard to notice the subtlety of his mood swings. I had lifetimes of practice scanning others' energy and emotional temperature. The more I asked if he was okay, the more he tried to hide. This game of chess continued for months. I would hide the gun and get the children out of the house then go for a trip somewhere, usually to the beach. He'd confront me. I would lie, make up a story, and give him back the gun.

His internal storm was brewing The sign was a certain look in his eye, something he let only me see, hiding it well from others. It was a distant, lost look. His pupils looked like a black abyss. This darkness was supported by stiffness in his neck, and he'd recite the same story like a ritual. This story always ended with piercing punctuation. He romanticized how he had escaped death so many times in his life, only to end up wanting to end it himself. He'd share how he tried to do it, in the past, but how the image of his mother's pain kept him from squeezing the trigger. But after we moved to Florida, he started speaking in the present tense of how was planning to kill himself. It was a living nightmare. Groundhog Day every day, always the same thing.

We would sit outside on the patio or in our garage, two of his favorite places to exist. I positioned myself so I could see if the kids were coming, ready to run defense, if need be. I always preferred being the one to respond to them, if they needed anything, because I feared what he might do or say in response to them. Depending on his state of mind, the possibility of his delivered angry verbal attacks was high.

So, I sat as I usually did, part in fear and part lost, lonely and open to receive any sign of love he might be able to give.

He assumed a position almost hovering over the ground. He would pull a long drag from his cigarette, staring at the red ember, and then he'd begin.

Speaking from his nose, he whispered words about his projected death in the same way he'd recite the rosary. He made a gesture with his fingers like a gun and placed them to his temple, saying, "Here." Then, slowly and methodically, he would lower his hand, insert his fingers between his lips, and point them upward to the roof of his mouth, again muttering, "Here." As he stared right through my frozen face, he'd squeeze the imaginary trigger.

It didn't matter how many times he did it, my body always jumped, my eyes winced, and my heart sank. I was witness to his death every time he shared this, over and over again.

After he saw my reaction, he'd always say, "Don't worry, beautiful mama." He was going to go away, leaving me with the girls. "Out West, deep in the woods, where sound doesn't carry, so I can end myself of this misery in peace. And you won't have to suffer with my wretched, wretched existence anymore."

This was a double whammy to my heart. "In peace" meant I had some responsibility for his own internal war. *In peace,* as though our children's broken hearts were not a concern. *In peace.* It was all I wanted to be, and this was the furthest thing from it.

Every day was a battle, just walking from the car through the kitchen to our bedroom. Eggshells would have been welcome. Stepping on tacks would have been easier. This was a minefield. As I write this now, I see the greatest tragedy is, at that time, I believed I was somehow responsible for Andy's pain. I didn't want to be in this nightmare; I wanted to be a breath of fresh air. *His* breath of fresh air.

I thought back to the time I wrote little notes and scattered them throughout his home.

You are a miracle.

Your family loves you.

Here's to being one another's breath of fresh air.

I love you.

There was something within me that didn't want to give up. This conflict ran deep and affected any of my free will.

When he first told me the story of his attempts at suicide, they we're always relayed in the past tense. "His false self." His eyes would well with tears, and I'd feel his pain. My insides were wrung like a wet rag to see the magnitude of his sadness. And I felt a familiar despair, the way an old, sad song leaves a warm ball of metaphysical goo in the pit of your heart, no matter how many times you listen to it. Andy had a knack of creating this response in most anyone he met. He also magnified an ancestral connection to death, misery, and self-destruction that coursed through my family's veins. It felt like home.

But now, as his eyes teared up, something hit inside me differently. My aha moment revealed to me that in his tearful response was something I hadn't registered before now.

A God/universal moment of truth again.

The glasses of the universe were placed on my face, and I could see Andy. Not fully, but enough to peek behind the curtain that he, the grand wizard, hid. It was open enough that I clearly saw him moving the levers and cuing the drama, the manipulation, the pulling his subjects in really close. As he did, he'd sink in another hook without my noticing. The energy was thick. He was fully engaged and enthralled with his own performance, so much so that he, himself, was moved to tears. He. Was. Weeping. At. His. Own. Performance. Not at the experience.

I had flashbacks of other times when he'd reeled me in close only to completely gut me emotionally and then walk away, projecting back on me that there was something utterly wrong with me. They hit me hard. I felt like I was going to vomit.

The spirit I thought I had all but lost was awakening. I learned, once again, this universal wisdom and truth:

"You can't break a strong spirit. It is the spirit that breaks you through."

The fight I had within me became a fight for myself. Don't get me wrong: at many times in my life, my back has been up against the metaphorical wall, and I fought. Hard. But now, all of the work I had done for decades, all the resolve I had, and the circumstances in front of me changed my perspective. It superseded this war that, somehow, I had agreed to fight every day on his behalf.

The battle scenes inside of him were coming out, becoming more horrifying every day. Now, here was one where, somehow, I was responsible for preventing Andy from taking his life. He was using this as a way to control me. What the actual !*%?

The lava that churns within my belly is fueled by my wounds, both healed and unhealed. Ancestral wounds, the strength and wisdom of souls who came before me.

Everything about me was tired. I couldn't bear to look at my own reflection anymore. My entire emotional and physical state was exhausted, depleted, and defeated. But my spirit never fails me.

Like a lion's growl from deep within, I felt a rumble. It grew into a full and thundering growl. In the distance, I heard a "*Yip!*" A "*yip aye aye aye yeeeeee*" that erupted into a battle cry. Metaphysical swords and shields were raised as they guided me to start the charge forward. The metaphysical membrane that existed throughout my entire life was about to be pierced by generations of others who had carried the trauma until they could no more. I was ready for battle.

Many generations in my family have suffered deeply, and several have attempted to end their own lives, some successfully. Most of them who were on the receiving end of violence, abuse, denial, shame, and dogmatic persecution had watched from the ether, as I navigated through my own karmic minefield. It was they who suffered the original trauma of this particular strand of disease.

My grandfather and great-grandfather, my cousins, and my parents all did what they could to survive. Most of them found a way to survive and stayed in survival mode, while some ended their lives. But now, the heavy lift had somehow landed with me. The abilities to see, feel, project, heal, and transform were my greatest gift and my deepest pain. Like everyone before me, I was given the choice to barely survive or to burn this karma to the ground once and for all. I was given the tools and the responsibility to transmute this and make it the end of the line. To try to have it end with me.

All of my girls are highly gifted, able to communicate with and see the unseen. V walked into the living room and went directly to a photo of my grandfather, "Pop-Pop." She had never met him, looked at the photo, or asked about my family. He had passed when Elizabeth was a baby.

As V picked up the photo from the table, she said, "You can do it. Did he ever say, 'You can do it' to you?" Her face was relaxed, and she showed me that she was completely curious and surprised about being prompted to ask this question. She must have read the shock and surprise on my face, as well. She asked again, "Mom, did he?"

"Yes. Yes, he did. All of the time. Especially when I was younger, and Pop-Pop saw I was struggling, mostly in school and doing math. He would sit with me at my grandparents' kitchen table after dinner, and while my grandmother was organizing the kitchen for the next day, he would sit there, patiently and calmly showing me what to do. I would break down out of frustration, because the numbers kept transposing themselves and jumping off the page at me. I'd cry and say, 'I can't figure it out,' and every time, he would say, 'You can do it. You can do it. You can do it.'" Just like he was reading, *The Little Engine that Could*: "I think I can, I think I can."

When I was most frustrated, he would say to me, "I want you to say it with me--I can do it." By the end of the episode, I would be saying it and, literally, be doing it. My math and my climb.

Now, as V stood now directly in front of me, waving her hands at my face, I was in awe of the spirit. Just when I felt the most lost and alone, not knowing what to do because the circumstances of my life were jumping off the page, Pop-Pop came through. The trajectory of my life turned a few small notches that day. Just enough for me to start my exit plan. This exit took on all universal, ancestral, metaphorical, and cultural physical proportions.

I always felt a sense of collective responsibility and community, which I saw in the same strange way as even my husband did. It was part of what he had used to draw me in. I wanted to serve in bigger and greater ways as a healer.

However, I didn't discern the importance of seeing yourself as sacred first, before you began to help others.

You can't fill your emptiness through trying to make someone else full. You have to pour from a cup that you know holds power of your own potion. Because of Andy, I now see the difference. It was time for me to allow my well to be emptied and then go to an empty well and try to be fulfilled. It was time for me to heal this need to be needed.

"You can't save someone who isn't willing to participate in their own rescue."

When we still lived in New Jersey, a short time after Andy moved in with us, I started to notice his demeanor and personality shifting. I had walked in on his preaching angrily to my children, found pornography on our family computer, plus seen his secret messages to old girlfriends and new "friends." He'd started smoking weed (all night without sleeping) and more.

Whenever I talked to him about it, he asked me to help him learn how to be different. He always put me on a pedestal, saying I was one of the most powerful women he knew. It felt right to be the quiet voice standing behind him, helping him to navigate his stormy sea.

Over time, I spent many hours doing healing work on his physical, spiritual, and emotional planes. I helped him go to court and get full custody of his daughter, do his resume, organize his decades worth of poetry, and attempted to help him find peace within himself. He leaned on me for most everything. So much so that, when he was suffering, I didn't see where his pain began and mine could end.

And then I found myself alone again, much like during my first marriage, only now I had a third child who was suffering from reactive attachment disorder. I was taking care of our children while running a thriving business, going to horse shows, running singing lessons and therapy sessions, and fighting to keep the light bright in three confused, sensitive, and brilliant girls' eyes.

I regularly tried to communicate. I continued my own healing and therapy. I'd learned from my earlier mistakes, and I confronted the problem directly. It was the healthy choice. I'd tell him regularly how I felt, what I was experiencing, and what I needed. It turned a potentially healthy, uncomfortable conversation into a cyclical oration focused on my character. The dance of smoke and mirrors began. In the end, he never took responsibility for any of the things I mentioned, and he began to retaliate against me.

I inevitably had enough and told Andy to leave. He packed his things while letting out his most destructive verbal slicing and dicing, using against me all of the intimate and private hurts and vulnerability I had shared with him. He got in his car with V and told me he loved me, even though I was psychotic, haughty, misguided, and trying to be God. I was angry, stunned, and mostly confused.

The first time I kicked him out, I became physically sick. I wretched and vomited and passed out on my bed. Emily and Lizzy came in and lay with me while I apologized to them for everything that had happened. I was once again alone with the girls.

We lived in a house under foreclosure. Their father Tom, my husband of twenty-three years, had hidden many things from me, including not paying the bills, even though we made a sizable income. My attorney would ask,

"What does he *do* with all of this money?" I honestly didn't know.

My mother sat in the chair for my first appointment with her lawyer. She paid the retainer directly to Celine, who was quiet. I wondered if she'd heard a word that was said. My mother, despite all of our falling outs, was loyal to a fault and marched right up to the front and, without my asking, told me she was going to pay for the retainer. She made an appointment with her divorce attorney whom she'd used thirty years ago.

When I watched Andy drive away, I was immediately brought back to the day I'd asked my first husband to leave our marital home. It was after we had been separated for eight months.

While I was in Wyoming with Emily and Lizzy in a hotel room, preparing to go the airport to fly home, I received a text from Tom. It was short and to the point.

I found money that you were hiding in your dresser. Don't expect to find your truck here when you get home. I traded it in for a car for myself. I am leaving you the Subaru, which will be repossessed in a matter of days or weeks.

He stole five thousand dollars from my dresser, called off the mediator whom we had already paid for, to the finish of the divorce, and then he refused to sign. I responded to his text:

You are no longer welcome in the marital home. You have created a hostile environment for me and the girls, and I do not feel safe with you in the home. Be gone with all of your belongings by the time we return tonight.

I received his response when we landed.

I left four shutoff notices on the counter for you. Good luck with that.

I know you might think I can't be telling the truth. *How could I not know?* I was checked out, a workaholic, dissociated, and in full-on survival mode for years. I was surviving a life that I didn't want to be a part of. But I was too lost to know I had a choice to have a better one.

Until I got the strength to do something about it. I prepared myself and the girls by putting us all in therapy and starting a savings. I started a system to save that I lovingly call "Mike's Envelope System." My stepfather, Mike, told me he had purchased him first home, his cars, and his boat with cash he'd saved using his envelope system. So, I put my foot on the gas pedal of my business, filled an envelope with $1000, sealed it, and started another one, repeating that and never looking back. It was just a matter of time until I had enough.

For months, I never knew if we would come home to a padlocked door. Even though my attorney advised me to stay as long as I could, I knew we were on borrowed time. I was petrified. The girls didn't feel safe or have much interest in seeing their father. I often wondered how it had happened so fast. From owning a five-bedroom Colonial house and having a nest egg of savings, all our debt paid on a two-bedroom townhome, to this precarious living situation, wondering day to day how I was going to pull this thing off.

Until I reconnected with Andy.

I thought I had finally found true love. My body reacted to him with pure excitement and love. I felt a lump in my throat, and my heart pounded with anticipation. Or so I thought.

Our on again, off again push-pull became my normal.

Whenever Andy and I were apart, he sent me messages, music like, "Ain't no sunshine when she's gone" and other love poems. He called to say his shitty behavior and attitude were because he was just miserable living in New Jersey. According to him, it was a "Godforsaken state." He wanted to move to Florida.

I barely ate when he was gone. My body physically hurt, and I always felt better when he reached out. I was lost and in a constant state of confusion. I was a successful business owner, a well-respected and loved leader of my created community, adored my children, and yet I felt lost, depressed, unfocused, and distracted when Andy wasn't around.

Ultimately, we would reunite. The first few days and weeks after reuniting were always good. Then, he began to return to a dark place. He'd come home after work and appear distant. His body was always tense, and I'd try to switch up the energy by making gourmet meals, being home for him when he returned from work, and leaving him cards and love notes in his pocket to find as a surprise.

But I'd find him in bed, sleeping, with his hooded sweatshirt covering his head. I would lie with him while he slept. Praying. Enjoying the only peace we shared, as he slept. I'd look at his face and see the innocence return as he drifted off to his preferred place—anywhere but this place.

He would inevitably wake the next day and go to work, leaving without a goodbye most days. In the end, the message was clear in his words that I wasn't doing things right or enough, and he was too overwhelmed to take care of anything to do with V. He continued to withhold affection, attention, and information. I asked if we could see a counselor for help. We saw a priest at the church where his father was the former deacon. He encouraged us to seek further guidance from a professional, which we did until she asked to see me alone.

Her eyes were soft as she peered at me from her comfy chair. "How are you managing, Shar?" she asked.

I thought it odd that she'd called me that, considering she hadn't done so before. She smiled as she asked, "Do you know what you are taking on?"

Blinking far too many times as the wall of isolation and defense within me rose, I mouthed, "I do."

"Well, if you want to continue to see me, it will have to be alone. This setting is not appropriate for your husband." She told me she wasn't comfortable seeing us as a couple, but I was welcome to continue.

I don't recall the rest of the exchange. I was fully dissociated. I was back in isolation. In the cave, preparing for a long journey of restriction and lack. A different type of walking meditation. I knew it well. It was my comfort zone. I had become very good at appearing like I was present, even when I was far away, gathering wood, building my wall, preparing for battle.

Deep, deep within, I knew exactly what it was the therapist had asked me to see, what I was taking on. The wound within me begged for healing and was asking for me to take the journey inward. Instead, I was seeking to find the worthiness and love I had not received from someone who could not give it. It's all I knew. Without knowing I did.

The dichotomy of the vibrational existence of a martyr (me) and a faithful person in service (her), who was asking for help of others who were in religious service. The parts of us that greeted each other were so deeply programmed, as women, under the structured institution of religion and so misaligned that we missed the opportunity to truly be of service.

The evidence of divine truth is never far behind. We must lift our eyes upward and inward, if we want to see truth.

Within moments after that, the secret messages to women returned, along with drunken nights with our neighbors. I'd seen it enough times to know that it mattered not what lives he traumatized along the way. He blamed me for being brainwashed by the therapist. He called me weak for being so impressionable, and egotistical for caring about a business, my business, that served the "spoiled, entitled rich"

Andy had no social awareness. No feedback changed his course. He was aggressive, irrational, and oppositional with anyone whom he thought was "off-center."

One night, driving home with our little family in the car, he started a fight with a van that had somehow managed to catch his paranoid eye. He tried several times to run them off the road. He opened my window to throw a full can of soda at their windshield. He was driving at 80 miles an hour.

We all sat paralyzed. I muttered the words, "Please, stop. Please think about the children. They are in the back seat, petrified."

Whatever poison he had left was poured directly into me. I thought I was strong enough to take on his darkness. I thought I had helped him heal the things he told me hurt him. But it seemed as though, each time I worked on him, he became more venomous.

I longed for the man who had stood over me while I slept, thanking God for me. The one who said he'd met his wife after the first time we spoke. I kept thinking about the times and ways he had poured his love into me. The way he'd said he couldn't live without me. The things he'd written to me. I kept trying to create scenarios where he'd *see me* as the person he wanted and had said he needed me to be. I was performing to create the circumstances for him to feel fulfilled and relaxed enough to go back to that love again.

I gave up hope and realized there was nothing within him that showed remorse for the pain he caused me, my children, and his daughter. After I put the girls to bed, I grabbed the keys to my car and drove past the general store and over the mountain to the next town over. I had to create distance.

It was pouring rain, and the windshield wipers couldn't keep up with the dousing storm. Frustrated, I couldn't drive any farther. I felt trapped in a web.

I pulled onto a side street and, without warning, let out a blood-curdling, soul-crying scream. I didn't recognize the sound of my own voice. I sounded like a cross between a wild hyena and lion. I screamed and punched the steering wheel until I was able to cry. I was so numb I couldn't even cry without punching my fist on something, punching. through the membrane of my own protection. But once broken, my heart and I sobbed.

I hadn't had a moment without anyone hearing me. I hadn't had a moment to connect with myself. I was in constant work mode, from the moment I woke until I passed out from the day.

I confronted Andy, and he told me he wanted to move. We decided we would move to Florida. I thought it was to save our new marriage. To help his quality of life.

When she heard the news, Andy's sister called to tell me her brother wasn't welcome there. He had caused enough pain in all of their lives. I told him this. I'm not sure I gave any thought to what she said, however, because Andy had already explained that his sister was an irrational, spoiled, and jealous woman who was heavily reliant on their parents. His mother was always gracious, and his father provided caution and boundaries for his son to keep in mind when we moved there. It seemed odd to me.

It took a few weeks for him to go from incredible to miserable, which weighed heavily on all of us. I tried to protect the children as much as I could and took on more responsibilities, so he would be less stressed.

We packed everything I owned and could fit in a U-Haul to move to Florida. We left the house and the rest of the belongings inside it. Our neighbors helped us pack and later came to take their pick of our remaining possessions, like vultures on road kill. I tried to think of this as the beginning of a fresh start. Again. I had lost almost everything I had worked for, plus walked away from my well-established and successful business on a promise of things getting better. I was afraid, but I surrendered to the notion of saving our marriage. I was determined to not let this become a failure.

The twenty-hour drive was ominous. Lizzy was shell-shocked. I was paralyzed and faking positivity to prevent a blow out before we landed in Andy's self-proclaimed Mecca.

The first days in Florida helped create the clarity around what I feared most. The move further isolated me, while he got worse by the minute. The storm I knew in New Jersey was nothing compared to the existence that was Andy in Florida.

He had alienated me from most of my family and friends and isolated us from our neighbors; one couple even moved away, claiming they were petrified of him. He came to my job and threatened my boss, resulting in my being fired. Lizzy, who was traumatized and psychologically tortured by him told me she was leaving to see her father for a month. I knew the moment she left that she was not going to return.

On this day, I felt a new shift and knew something was different. When I did, I decided I'd choose a different path altogether. I realized the fight for Andy's life had now become the fight to reclaim mine.

As I listened once again to his oration, telling me of his self-destructive plan, I looked him in the eyes and said, "You are in the depths of a storm of your own darkness. This is yours to fight for, and you are spreading this around like poison to everyone. You are waiting to hit rock bottom to turn yourself around, and that isn't going to happen. *Ever!!*"

I continued, "You have tried to pull me in. Don't you see? I cannot help you by joining you in your darkness. I can't help you by trying to help you out of there. I cannot stay here as a bystander, watching you drown. I am tossing you a rope to help you out. *Take the rope, damnit.*"

TAKE. THE. ROPE.

"You *must* get help."

I read him the poem he'd written me when we first reconciled and, defeated and numb my legs carried me away. I refused to let him see me crying. I was done with letting him see any effect on my life. No more. Not another tear.

Though I hoped he would seek help and change, I knew chances were slim, and after his living a lifetime feeding his disease, it might be too late.

From that point on, I tried to do everything I knew to help. Called his parents, therapists, spiritual counselors, couples counseling, family intervention, my own healing.

Nothing could penetrate his pathology. His soul was buried down so deep and was consumed by this darkness.

Every single person he saw said the same thing to me. "What's your exit plan?" Every person held on to hope that maybe now would be the time he would turn to walk toward the light.

But as soon as he was requested to be accountable for his behavior or to grow, things got worse and beyond ugly. Then he took it out on me and our children.

A spiritual counselor saw us weekly. We met at a park. Andy, contrary to our requests and the state boundaries for our sessions, came high and had been drinking. He brought a forty-two-ounce filled with gin and tonic cup to a session.

We walked the sidewalk to our meeting spot, and when he saw Jennie, he immediately grabbed my hand and kissed it for effect. That was the first time he had touched me all day. I remained mute. He had taught me there would be painful retaliation for my being open in our sessions. So, I smiled at Jennie and sat at the picnic table while he stood behind me.

Jennie began our session and watched Andy with concern. He was visibly angry and animated as he spoke aggressively about me and about how much I was "off-center and disrespecting him." He used terminology she had shared in past sessions as ammunition against me. He paced around behind me as he spoke, which I could hear through the pinging of his voice off the canopy behind us. Though I had grown terrified of him, I knew his energetic patterning and movement like I knew my own.

When his eyes were averted, Jennie glanced toward me and mouthed, "Are you okay?" I just stared through her. I knew enough not to respond. Andy would know. I had no fight left in me and used my energy to duck and swerve around the licks of energy as he lashed out.

Jennie confronted him about drinking that night. But before she could finish, he denied it, saying he was fully sober and crystal clear.

"Crystal clear to see through the bullshit," he spat.

She flinched but persisted and asked him to let her smell his cup.

His presence loomed large, and he exploded at us both. As Andy turned his attack to Jennie, I sat there, seeing yet another source of hope and help turn to dust. Though most of what he said is a blur to me, because I dissociated, I can still feel my way through the moment. He brushed past me and, without turning to look, said, "Come on, Mama."

I don't know how long I sat. I was barely there, frozen. I stared at the crossroads in front of me, not knowing what to do next.

Jennie broke the silence and looked at me with eyes that had seen much more than most. In her thick Southern drawl, she said calmly, "It's time to create your exit plan. You've got to get yourself and Lizzy out. *Now*." She knew this darkness well. For she openly admitted that this situation, in many ways, *was* her, until she fully surrendered to her healing and to God. "What is your exit plan, Sharon? What is your plan?"

I flashed back to our first meeting together. We had connected through Celebration Church, a church I had started to attend when a neighbor told me about it. I went alone, and the first time I attended, I was skeptical. There was music blaring outside Celebration and the bass was thumping as I climbed the Art Deco staircase into a stadium.

The lights went dark, and the band began to play, "Behold (Then Sings my Soul)." A woman's angelic voice sang, "This is my soul, this is my soul. How great your love is. This is my soul."

The words were displayed on a large screen on the stage. I sang them in my full singing voice, knowing that nobody could hear me in a full auditorium with concert-level volume and sound systems. I immersed myself fully, swaying my body, feeling the sounds vibrate within and throughout. I sang from the depths of my belly, "Speaking truth when I can't find it," as though it was my bedtime story. I was putting yet another one of my nightmares to bed. I felt the familiar touch of the wise one who knows, and my body crumbled into a surrendered blessed, messy mess. I stood in the dark of the 5000-seat auditorium with my hands raised above my head, full on crying, as I sang the words in full declaration, "This is my soul."

Tears flooded down my face until my shirt was fully soaked, physical evidence of the complete shifing of my body, mind, and spirit. I knew it was a divine intervention. The intercession was much-needed.

Funny that it came through the one church my father-in-law and second husband mocked and resisted. In my rebellion and desperation for connection to my higher power, I found out when services were and went. I silently said my thanks. *Thank you for holding me, thank you for finding me, thank you, ancestors, for your strength, and thank you for this dark auditorium, so no one sees me coming fully undone.*

Being filled by the music of the gospel in this church on this day was what I'd needed. It was as close to the magic I knew in this lifetime. The following day, I called the director of outreach and asked for help. I was fully screened and referred to Jennie. She and I met alone first, and I waited until the right time to ask Andy to attend sessions.

"You are and always will be divinely protected. In all ways always. When you take one step toward the direction of your health and higher self, God gives you ten."

Still, it was a rough road. Still, it was nothing like the depths of his abyss. I enlisted Jennie to help. Shocked, he agreed to attend. We had sessions for a few weeks before this evening when he walked off. Now, just like with the spiritual counselor, the psychotherapist, the priests, and the psychiatrist, it was over.

My hope of him getting better was completely lost. I sat there, thinking about the years I had spent dreading going home to my parents' house, a fear and dread deep within the pit of my stomach. I recalled the familiar pain of feeling alone, unseen, and unsafe. No matter how many years ago and no matter the miles away, no matter the strength I had built to endure my life, I had not outrun my past or my origin. The shame I felt was palpable.

This moment I learned the living example to: "Get ahold of and heal your past, before it grabs ahold of you."

Staring at the table, I took a deep breath.

My eyes rose first, rolling upward and willing my body to join, as I stood up from the picnic table bench. My head felt disconnected and floating above it all. I straightened my shoulders and grabbed my purse with my eyes fixed forward toward the sidewalk, where he and I had made our manufactured entrance. I nodded and thanked Jennie and then walked like a zombie to the car.

Andy was standing outside of the driver's door, smoking. Fully knowing he wouldn't let me drive, I got in the passenger seat, with my neck straight and my eyes forward. I fought like hell to stay present in my body as he drove. The air was thick and dark with anger.

I wish I could tell you what I did on that drive home. I hope I prayed. I hope I asked for guidance. I hope I asked for protection of my children. But I know overall I braced myself for his wrath, an all too familiar feeling, my coping tools at the ready.

I was grateful Emily was safely tucked away in college. Though heartbreaking, I was also grateful Lizzy was with her father. Part of my prayer was answered in the form of the most piercing heartache. The only saving grace and motivation were my daughters. I loved them fiercely, though perhaps misguided and egotistically. My daughter Lizzy was tired of the emotional roller coaster we rode, with my leaving and then staying and then leaving again, only to devastate her with my decision to stay. She had conspired to leave a few weeks prior, feigning a visit with her father. I felt it in my bones that she wouldn't return.

I flashed back as I sat in her room while she packed her things, her uncomfortable silence tripping the wire for me. My heart ached. I knew she was leaving. The once little girl who had to be peeled from my side had to leave her mother because I had married and was somehow in love with a madman.

I knew she was going through a tremendous amount of pain by how pronounced her tics were and by the return of her skin picking. She had packed more than a vacation required, though much less than a full exit.

Emily had flown down to bring her sister to New Jersey. Em, Lizzy, V, and I went through the motions together for a few days. We were all numb, confused, traumatized, tired, and distant. We all knew our lives were going to dramatically change forever in the weeks to come. Though I was a shell of my former self, I still fought like hell to be able to provide for my children.

But at that moment and in the moments that followed, the only fight I had was used to fight back tears as I hugged them both at the airport. I numbly stood as I watched my two reasons for living go through security. My two little warriors were going back to base camp. I was relieved they would be safe. I was heartbroken that this whole mess was happening. I was lost because the only identity I had that I was proud of was being their mom.

I'd wanted to be nothing like my parents when I had my own children. Yet here we were, feeling such deep pain and betrayal without the ability to find the words to say it.

Turning back once more to wave, I blew them both kisses. I did my best to smile. Because this unspoken truth cut deep. They knew, I knew, he knew, and not a word was spoken. Head fixed, I rotated my body. Turned on my heel to walk away and can't remember much of the days afterward.

I spent most of my time isolating. I would sit in the bedroom in shock, numb, and listening for movement in the house. While I was scrolling through Facebook and reclining on the bed, Andy entered the room with a plate and set it on the dresser. My body started to shake. Andy chuckled to himself and muttered something I couldn't translate. His eyes fixed on the television as he slowly chewed a piece of pizza and gently wiped his mouth.

"What are you laughing about?" I asked.

In his dismissive monotone voice, he said, "Wow, I laugh and you start the psychodrama once again."

I sat up, my body at 10 on the Richter Scale of tension. My voice shook as I stammered, "I asked you what you are laughing and muttering about under your breath."

I knew I needed to see what I needed to see, so I pressed and waited. We sat in the thick of this darkness for what felt like hours.

Andy kept his eyes forward, looking into the abyss, and slowly hissed, "I'm laughing, thinking about how I'm going to kill you. I'm going to shoot you between the eyes while you sleep." And then, as monotone as his voice, his exit hummed as he walked out of our bedroom.

My entire body jolted when I heard him say, "V-bot! what you doing, beautiful?"

Every storm that comes to pass is not yours to fix.

It was time to plan my exit. I had tried everything within my power to help, and now I had no choice but to leave. To walk away from everything I owned once again. I couldn't bear being away from my children. Somehow, I think they knew it or were carried by their own angels, but they saved my life by leaving. They saved our lives by making the most painful decision to remove themselves from the toxicity and chaos. They saved my life by disconnecting their tie to me.

I decided that night that every single thing I had experienced in my life that could have destroyed me, and that nearly did, I had survived. It changed me in unspeakable ways, most of them causing me to armor up in such a way that I hid more of myself. I was ready to learn a different way to move through things I never thought I'd have to overcome.

I was raised to believe I had to fix others. To take on their pain in order to be worthy. It's why I was so drawn to people who were in so much pain. I subconsciously believed it was my only way to exist. My worth was tied to the result of helping others in their storms, many of whom created their own chaos to weather. I learned that I was never meant to take on others' pain. I was not here to fix their storm. Finally, I learned that I didn't want to anymore.

I was there to learn what I needed to do to get strong for myself. I no longer wanted to be a wounded healer. I flashed back to a past life where I was murdered by a patron because I'd refused to take his pain into my body. This was the insight I needed now, to realize this was part of what I was here to heal in this lifetime. I wasn't at all prepared, because I had allowed someone else to disable me completely, but I was ready, because I had trained lifetimes for this.

V used to question me about her father.

"Why is he *so mean*? Why is he so *angry* all the time, and why doesn't he change? He's hurting you. And me. He scares me. And I don't think Lizzy will ever come back. Do you?"

At age nine, she was so intuitive. She saw the look on Lizzy's face when she left, and she saw me check out. She cried to me, saying, "Are you leaving? You promised you'd never lie to me. You have to tell me. Are you going to leave? Because if you are, I'm coming with you. I already lost my first mom. I can't lose you. You are my real mom. I prayed for you. I love you. *You can't leave me.*" And the once little feral child looked like a beautiful fairy. She took her sticky hands and put them on my face, just as she had the first night we met on her birthday, with her big teeth and beautiful brown eyes filled with tears. "Promise you won't leave me behind with him. I'm scared." The same scared she had been when we hid in her room as we heard her mom outside, yelling. The same shaking she had experienced when she was petrified to see her mother, when she was showing up.

I looked at her and said, "I won't lie to you. I'm not sure, V. I don't know how much longer I will be able to stay." That was the best I could do in that moment. Any more and I would jeopardize my safe exit.

She ran to her room, and when she slammed the door and, a picture frame fell onto the floor.

So many people were crushed in Andy's ambling storm.

My experience in his hurricane goes beyond being traumatized. It was a wreckage of epic proportions.

Words cannot do justice to explain this existence. My body signaled something that my brain called love. This was love as I knew it. It hurt. It would make me physically sick. It would make me cry. It was slowly chipping away at the person I thought I was. It felt familiar. Seven generations back had seen to it that I knew what it felt to know love and fear, as a bonded, hurtful pair.

⚫●◆◆●⚫

I already knew I had to leave, and I was measuring out how. Not unfamiliar, I was alone in this. My brain was constantly bouncing to different scenarios and possible exits.

Until my friend Bonnie called. Unlike most times since I'd married Andy, I answered the phone. We had met twenty years prior, in Clarksville, Tennessee, when our then husbands were stationed at Fort Campbell in Kentucky. We became fast friends and had some of the most hysterical and bizarre moments during our time there. We were known for starting a full-on laugh fest in a car full of people, having strange allergic reactions to food that skirted death, and sharing a Thanksgiving turkey that left us all thankful for not getting salmonella (because I forgot to remove the giblet bag).

Our friendship wasn't based on platitudes. It was built on authenticity and life on life's terms. We are strong women who were married to active service-minded (and self-centered) alpha men. I remember saying goodbye when I moved from Tennessee. We were both without words, but our tearful hug said enough.

We had souls that were destined to live larger than life and a deep knowing that our friendship was the kind that stands the test of time. Over the years, we shared in the birth of the six beautiful children we collectively had and made trips to see each other as often as we could.

Bonnie is full of personality and has content delivery down to a science. She is one of few people I know who can tell a story uninterrupted. I said, "Hi," and from 1500 miles away, she energetically reached through the phone to cover my mouth and left no oxygen for me to say another word, her New England accent pronouncing my name like "Cher."

"Now, don't try and pretend everything is okay. I want to talk to you, and I need you to go somewhere where you can. Now, Shar." She has a way of showing her emotions by contracting her throat and speaking through her teeth as she delivers her message. I've heard this more than a few times in our nearly thirty years of friendship. I knew enough was enough.

My body was tired, my heart terrified, and my mind at a loss for intelligence. I had been in a war zone for years and was in the peak of battle.

I snuck out of the house like a rebellious teenager at midnight on a school night. Andy was drinking a forty-eight-ounce gin and tonic while watching TV and didn't notice I'd left. Scared and hopeful, I parked my car in a parking lot a mile away and brought her up to speed as best I could. Bonnie listened, took notes on the priorities, and then paused a long pause.

I could hear her swallowing. Maybe buying time, so she could push away the lump in her throat. I could tell her head was down, her chin to chest, as I heard her say, "Leave it all. I'm buying you a plane ticket to Connecticut. You are leaving. To-night."

No.

No-no-no-no-no.

I couldn't do that. There was important paperwork, my children's entire lifetime of artwork, and the last living thing that kept me close to my girls, our beagle bulldog, Penny. There was no way I would leave any of these things behind. I had already lost so much: My entire home in New Jersey, with its furnishings, everything I'd worked for, sentimental objects, and now my children.

"I have to be calculated about this. Most of the time, he is in some sort of psychosis. I can't do it when he is home." I also had no one there to help me. Andy saw to it that every friendship I made was lost. I had to do this all on my own.

She pressed me to change my mind. "Listen, I know you aren't planning on staying, but I don't want to have to read about your death in the paper and plastered all over the media. You're not going out this way! No, Shar. You don't seem to realize what you are dealing with here."

"I know I'm in danger." As my tongue clicked the roof of my mouth, my body resonated with a thump. It was the first time I had said it out loud. This was what I needed to feel, know, and accept. I was in too deep and was now in danger. I had gone too far, trying to take on someone else's journey. So much so that I'd had to call my father and tell him what was happening.

The most power you have is to change your own life. Denial is a main coping mechanism for people within generational trauma. By stopping the use of this coping method, we can be seen as the problem. But in reality, we are breaking the cycle of trauma and suffering.

I had to face the truth. My karmic lesson in denial and facing the truth intersected with my father's own karma of expectations, codependency, and illusions. He needed me to be the problem child. So much so that for most years his Christmas letter sent to his family and friends made no mention of me.

My father saw this as another way that I was a problem. I was flawed and admitting it. I was finally fully committed to speak authentically about my experience. I was also fully aware that the narrative was going to be manipulated by him and my mother, once they connected and discussed this. I was willing to exist in that space so I could leave this one. But I was not willing to continue to be the secret keeper for any of the toxic relationships I have in my life.

Andy was asked to work overnight, and I knew it was go time. I packed my GMC Denali SUV with anything I could stuff into the back. Important paperwork, financial documents, birth certificates, all of my children's artwork from birth to now, Breyer horses, clothing, and dog food.

It was midnight, and I thought she was asleep, but V was awake in her room. I should have known that her sensitivity to emotions and energy would tip her off.

She appeared in the office with tears brimming her eyes. Looking at me and then to where I was preparing a bin, she said, "Mom, you are leaving... Mom, look at me.

Please tell me that you're taking me." She started to move my piles of papers as part of her fight against this.

My silent response filled any shadow of doubt that she was wrong.

Fully sobbing, she said, "I love you, Mom. I can't lose you. I don't want to live with Dad! I want to stay with *you*. You are my real mother. I need you to help me with everything! *MOM!*" Her skinny arms flailed toward me.

I carefully set down the papers in my hands and opened my arms. I love her so much. V fell into them and wept, muttering the same words over and over. "Take me with you. Please. My sisters. Mom. I need you."

I held my heartache back enough to say, "My little V, you were born in my heart, and that is where you will stay always. Things are messy right now, and I have to go. Tonight. When Dad comes home, I will leave. I've already called Amber, and she said she will let you stay there, if you need to. Even though there will be a distance between us, I will always be here for you. I will always leave a trail for you to find me, if you need me. No matter what Dad tells you, in the time I am away, always know I love you so much. I always will."

She sobbed until she had nothing left. Totally empty, she was exhausted. I tucked her into bed, finished my packing, and lay on top of the comforter of my bed to rest. Not one part of me wanted to lie any closer to his essence. He tried to Facetime me, and I ignored the calls. He wouldn't stop, and I fell asleep to the buzzing of my phone.

Andy came home, I heard the garage door open, and like I was a five-year-old girl, I pretended to be asleep.

Minding where he was, I listened intently to his footsteps, as I lay still.

He walked into the bedroom and said, "I knew you'd leave. I always knew you would. *You thankless bitch!*" He caught himself and composed himself. "You are the only one I loved. My heartfelt breath. I can't live without you. I can't take care of V without you. I can't do life without you. Please stay. Give me a chance."

I got up without speaking and attempted to go to the bathroom. At every step, he blocked me. Always careful before this not to touch me, he dropped his precautions and grabbed my wrists, holding them with my hands facing down in front of my body. I was glad I had mentally prepared myself for this as much as I could. But nothing prepared me for the internal response to this within my body.

His mouth shaped as though he was crying, his eyes dry without tears. Andy said, "Why are you doing this to me? Don't. Don't do this." When he lessened the grip on my hands, I shook them free and darted away.

As I moved to the right, he shifted to block me again. As he went to grab me, I reached my hand away and snatched my jeans. I ran into the bathroom and locked the door. Hopping on one foot, I shimmied into the pants, which, in turn, helped me armor and activate some logic within my mind.

"Okay, you can do this. If you play this right, in a few minutes, you will be in your car driving away. If he follows, you will speed, and a cop will pull you over, and you will ask them for help. You can do this. You have to do this" I thought of Emily and Elizabeth and swung the door open.

He was outside the door, leaning on the sink. I looked at his face. He had replaced his mask with the one I'd fallen in love with. "How does he do this? What am I doing?"

It hurt. This hurt. I was grieving the death of something I didn't fully grasp yet. But I did know that I needed to go. Love didn't have any space to live here. The only chance of him getting and participating in help was without me being his dumping ground.

His mask was still in place when I raised my eyes to his. "I know you don't understand this," I said. "I know you don't want me to leave. But this is the greatest act of love I could ever choose. Staying isn't going to help anyone and will hurt everyone." As I walked out, I was shocked that he didn't grab me. My back was arched just the same.

He yelled, "You don't know what the fuck you are doing! You are a liar. God is going to bring down His wrath on you."

I got Penny in the car, started the engine, and slowly drove out of the driveway. When I looked in my rearview mirror, I saw both him and V standing in the middle of the road. I shouted into the mirror at my eyes, to them, and back to my eyes. "This is the lifetime that your soul breaks free! This is the lifetime that your soul breaks free. This is the lifetime that your *soul breaks freeeeee!*"

I drove a few miles away and pulled down a dirt road. Before putting the car in park, I fell apart. Completely undone. I was in complete and full shock. But I knew I had to move. I had to feel the tires rolling underneath me.

Penny knew, too. She felt the energy shift and stood on her hind legs to peer out the window. My co-pilot was ready to roll. I thanked God I had her with me, put the car in gear, and drove to the highway. *North will do. North is where my girls are. North is where I will create the space within myself to finally feel home.*

With every mile, the flashing white lines of the highway validated my independence from that life. Every so often, I peered back to be sure he wasn't following me. But every inch was an inch closer to my healing and my life. I strongly felt the presence of my Granny Marie and Pop-Pop, hearing "you can do it" as the miles rolled on.

I started the process of discovering my home. Determined that this lifetime would be the one when my soul breaks free. At a rest stop, I messaged a therapist I was following on social media who talked about interpersonal violence, narcissistic abuse, and healing.

I wrote: *I think I might be in an abusive relationship. I just left and am on the road, literally driving away from it all.*

While waiting for a response, I wrote "Departure."

Departure

"This is the greatest act of love one could ever choose."
—My parting words as I left

Branding prayers and love on your face like a mother kissing her baby's cheeks, I view you from my rearview mirror. Shouting over and over in a voice reminiscent of my own, "This lifetime will be the one your soul breaks free."

    I say this for you. I say this for me. ~SJL.

CHAPTER EIGHT

FORGIVENESS

"We must give up hope for a different past and focus our efforts on the opportunity of a better future."

There is no greater moment than when you raise your head above the rubble of the life you are buried under and choose to forgive. From ancient mysticism and religious context to theology and philosophical texts, we are shown the positive effects created by the choice to forgive. Forgiving yourself and others has become one of the most sacred and spiritual acts in our own transformation and transcendence.

But most of us don't truly embody the true act of forgiveness. Sadly, this means we perpetuate disease. Divine spiritual wisdom teaches us that disease is a conflict between two forces. In the Tao, it's yin and yang fighting against each other rather than dancing with each other. In ancient mysticism, it's the dance of the dark and the light. In science, it's the fight between form and matter against flow.

When we want to forgive out of fear of the loneliness, being lost, being discarded like trash, etc., by seeing the truth, we are continuing to deepen the illusion that attachment likes to create. We shove our intuition and the communications from our soul deep down into our physical body in order to prevent further hurt. Our body become heavy, and further conflict occurs until it gets so loud, it affects us viscerally.

We must find ways to let go of our experiences. Forgiveness is alchemy.

Forgiveness can stay in the queue as we wait for someone to admit something they've done in direct relation to you. But you are the only one who can step aside from the waiting line and say my favorite saying in healing: "FTS." Fuck that shit.

One of the most disempowering things we can do is to let anything in our lives hinge on another's actions. You give others your precious energy when you focus on them. On their pain. Their disease. Their actions. You are the greatest alchemist of your life. What if you used the powerlessness and victimhood that you may have been forced to experience as the catalyst to birth yourself into the world as your full self?

No more suffering.

No more hiding.

No more accepting someone else's opinion of you as truth.

When we've experienced trauma in early life, we have a tendency to stay stuck in the phase where we look to others to explain our worth. "Mommy, look at this picture I drew." Or, "Dad, come watch me spiral this ball." We hinge on our parents' responses to tell us if we are good enough, doing enough, strong enough.

When you are born into this physical body, you are not guaranteed that the parents you have will be your wise counsel. Society tells us they should be. But spiritual guidance tells us this isn't always in alignment.

It is up to you alone to discover your own truth.

How, you ask. By going on an inward journey, body-mind-spirit. The journey is much like climbing a never-ending mountain: no fancy gear; just yourself. You never know what you'll find. The conditions of the land and its inhabitants will dictate the challenge. Your own unique expression is what creates the outcome and potential alchemy for you and the collective world around you.

Only if you are willing to open your metaphysical eyes to the truth of the truth. No more hiding. You must organically rise into your truth without force or manufacturing anything. By forgiving, shame will dissipate, and you will no longer be bound to the experience or person of your trauma. You can stride forward in the divinely protected bubble of light, peace, and love.

You can help to heal traumatic experiences and ancestral trauma by forgiving. It literally burns the space held by a marker holding its place within your personal history. By understanding this divine spiritual wisdom, you realize the infinite power you possess. By breathing life into your own personal forgiveness, you not only liberate your own soul, you liberate the souls of seven generations behind and to come.

There are steps to our forgiveness that are necessary. First, you must be aware of the truth and your personal truth. For you, this may be easy. For me, it was difficult, though not for reasons you might think. I wasn't holding a grudge; I just didn't know how tainted the lens was that I looked through. I had no idea that things I found normal wasn't healthy. Things like living in survival mode, allowing others full access to me, defending myself to others, performing for acceptance, being the object of my mother's anger, comparison, competition, and living in constant physical pain.

I also didn't know why I had had the belief most of my life that, on some or all levels, I really didn't exist. How could I even understand my worth, when I didn't understand the energetic impression of my soul here on this plane? I was raised to believe that I existed only when I was doing something for others.

I'm sure this wasn't a conscious choice by any of my caregivers and parents. But to be a child of parents who were in toxic relationship with themselves, unable to receive feedback, unable to see the hurt they were creating by using me and others to feel better about themselves, neglecting to protect me, gaslighting, psychological abuse, and warfare, was enough to leave me like a wide-open receiver for further abuse, neglect, and mistreatment.

Not having the witnesses, AKA extended family, friends, and neighbors, step in and say no gives the vibration to our cells and nervous system that no matter how deep the cut, your safety and wounding are never going to be as equally or more important than another's sickness or belief.

Rewriting this is no easy task. But it is worth every ounce of effort. Things our caregivers and parents experience, like unhealed trauma, genocide, slavery, oppression, economic inequality, addiction, narcissism, and personality disorders most definitely affect our view of normal. Body, mind, spirit. So, in the end, the message we arrive at is that we are the only one with our unique fingerprint.

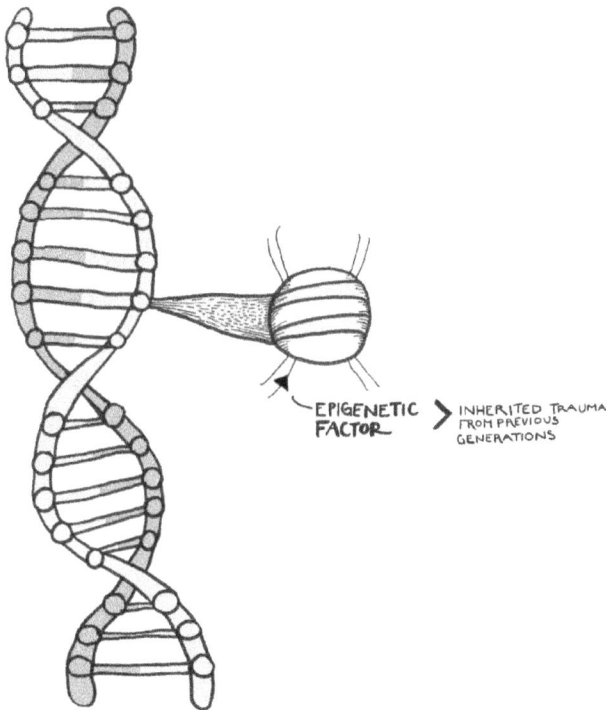

EPIGENETIC FACTOR > INHERITED TRAUMA FROM PREVIOUS GENERATIONS

Strengths as well as "wounds" by unhealed trauma are passed behaviorally and genetically through epigenetics. When you heal and work through your trauma, you heal it for previous generations. By healing, you choose not to pass it on to future generations.

You were birthed into this world to grow, thrive, and live in the truth and wisdom of your highest and best. We can gain so much wisdom by studying our ancestry, which is not to excuse how you have been wounded; rather, it's to understand the spiritual meaning of your own truth. From that truth, you can start to remove yourself from the enmeshed fibers and clearly see *you*, in your sacred space, and others in theirs. Your parents are on their own sacred journey, too. You can love them for the path they chose, understanding the challenges of a soul, their souls, existing and expressing through the human condition and form.

As with anyone with whom you intersect, you can choose forgiveness and acceptance. Knowing that you're on your journey and they are on theirs, you gain access through the unknown. You can love someone, you can have compassion for them and for your differences; you can be curious about their choices, so you can see them truly without understanding why and wholly forgive.

It's by divine design that we are here. By raising your eyes beyond the wound, you will find the meaning of your purpose and existence. It takes you from confusion to clarity, invisible to vision, suffering to surrender. Our world mirrors this in the language I have spoken for lifetimes: quantum metaphysics. Mysticism and pillars of health through healing have been my beacons.

The universal law of metaphysics shows us that flight is not possible without weight. The weight of the container has to be equal to the metaphysical energy lifting it. This energy responds to what is inside of you as much as what goes on around you. Thrust must be present for forward motion but is not possible without a drag or pull.

Plenty of things in my life were heavy and actively and intentionally tried to hold me down and back. It is the existence of these things that helped me create my own flight school. Throughout my life as an international healer, performance coach, and therapist, I have taught many other dragons and warriors how to fly. If I kept myself focused on my pain within the experience, I would remain stuck in what was meant to be a quick transition from my transmutation. Part of why I'm here is to help the collective heal from narcissistic abuse and all forms of trauma. The many-layered intersections of our minds, souls, bodies, and energy. Had I kept myself focused on the injustice of my own wounding, I would not have found and lived in my highest expression. I also would not have had the pleasure of working with the most gifted and wounded souls, so they could do the same. Forgiveness turned the key.

So, when I say you discover who you truly are by following the sacred act of forgiveness, I mean it in every literal and esoteric sense. You can finally see yourself as one. The self. The soul.

Your purpose and meaning are crystal clear when you stop looking directly at the person in front of you and, rather, look upward toward the multidimensional fractals of light to see the reflection of who is in front of you. It is then that our inward gaze becomes the catalyst for our self-love and compassion.

That's right. Forgiveness is sacred. You are sacred, even when you are surrounded by those who go out of their way to prove otherwise. If you've read this far, I want you to know that it is because of you being *you* that my life is richer. It's not your perfection that gives us joy. It is your expression. The more you rise into your highest self, even by a small percentage, you are helping to heal the world. You are a gift to the world and multiverse.

If a tree falls in the woods, and no one is there to witness it, does it make a sound?

If a narcissist is unable to see or hear you, do you truly exist?

I'm not ashamed to say I'm a late bloomer. I am also not ashamed to say I have gone from being my abusers' secret keeper and energy source to a dragon slayer's whisperer. You may have not heard any of my cries, but I know whoever needs to will hear me now.

I had two daughters who distanced themselves from me, I lost everything I owned twice, and I was burning down the remaining layers of disease that caused me to say yes to a sociopath. I had just come out from the closet. I was in a therapy session and had learned that the privacy I needed in my mother's home was as elusive as Big Foot. We can be in the woods and know he exists, but darn if we ever see them. The only privacy I knew was when I ran.

───────────●●●◆●●●───────────

I moved from the basement sofa with the baby snake and cave crickets to the second bedroom three quarters through my stay at my mother's. The closet was my safe space. My cocoon for the day. I was finally ready to emerge from both. Whether I intended to or didn't, *today* was the day.

I heard "*Shar!*" as my mother opened the bedroom door. She had on her interrogation face in full force, with her shoulders square and an off-putting look of disgust. Thinking she knew who I had been talking to, she stood poised to strike and barked, "Who were you talking to?"

My eyes were red and swollen, and my nose was raw from ninety minutes of blowing. Today had been a session full of heavy lifting and putting together the last pieces of transformation that came from seeing the truth of my circumstances. Truth in my previous marriage. Truth of my childhood, the trauma and its complexities intricately woven into my karmic wheel from my ancestors. The clinical lens calls this complex post-traumatic stress disorder or CPTSD. I call it transgenerational trauma and epigenetics and spiritual crisis.

I was today years old in therapy when I realized that my normal wasn't healthy. My healer and therapist had circled around this for months. That the trauma my mother experienced when she was pregnant with me, my parents' toxic relationship, led to unhealthy emotional manipulated by my parents. It is not healthy ever to be a pawn in parents' game of whose wound is bigger. To be in competition with or the subject of another's social paranoia. To be parentified by your abuser because they are having a breakdown. The list goes on.

To be in a state of survival and hypervigilance might be what you become accustomed to, but it is not how we are designed to live and stay within.

For most of my life, I treated anger like the plague. I grew up in a house full of anger, cutting communications, and hostility between my parents that ultimately fell on me and maybe my sister. The last thing I wanted was to be "like them," so I thought I was curing myself by never becoming an angry person. My chosen tools for survival were plentiful: people-pleasing, perfectionism, staying quiet and hypervigilant. I am no stranger to therapy and to seeking treatment for the immune diseases I developed as a result of trying to become immune to my painful upbringing. No one ever asked, "What happened to you?" No one was informed about my trauma.

It wasn't until my near fatal second marriage that I was able to find someone who was able to see. While in therapy, for months I fought being angry. I refused to say I was a victim of domestic violence. I didn't want to hear the words, let alone let them land. I was in denial. I didn't even know what a narcissist was.

My childhood was full of abuse, physical and psychological torture, neglect, and trauma. My adulthood and relationships were the result of my lack of understanding that both my parents were toxic, abusive, and neglectful. That doesn't mean they wanted to be; it just ended up that way. They, too, had deeply traumatic experiences with their parents that wounded the psyche. (That is their story to tell.) They did the best they could, but that was nowhere near what I needed.

I sought out the vibrational match of my childhood relationships and attachment/bonding within my intimate relationships. My husbands were never meant to love me. Only to teach me about myself and my lack of safety around intimacy and relationships.

I had no idea the depths this had affected me.

I started to seek deeper spiritual connection than ever before, plus healing and therapy, on the day I packed my car with my kids' artwork, which I had taken with me from home to home, the clothes, birth certificates, financial documents, and whatever else I could. I went to the bank and withdrew half of the last of what was left: $200. "My divorcé settlement," I thought.

I drove to Andy's parents' house to say goodbye, which was the best closure I could get. His father looked at me and said, "He's an idiot."

His mother said, "You have to do what is best for you and your girls." But neither of them could absorb how ill and dangerous their son was.

His father left the room and came back with $300. "Take care of yourself, and let us know when you arrive safe."

That was it. After trying four times, I was finally leaving. It took my daughter leaving and my friend telling me I was going to be killed, along with a vision of losing my teeth and having no way to see my children for me to see that I had to go in order to survive. The person who had promised to protect me turned into my greatest nightmare.

It felt strange to drive away, seeing the beautiful Florida sky behind me. When I stopped for gas or passed other cars, no one knew what I had just escaped.

I drove a thousand miles north with my beagle bulldog, Penny. My father found and paid for a hotel room, so I could sleep. I just lay there, buzzing. Flinching every time I'd hear a neighboring door close, knowing it was entirely possible he'd come find me.

"Inhale in your future, exhale out your fears." I focused on my breathing and did whatever I could to prepare for the next leg of my journey. Unfortunately, sleeping was not part of it.

As soon as I arrived in New Jersey, I went directly to my mother's house. I stepped out of the car, my feet on the driveway, and she ran out.

"Oh, my *God!*" my mother cried. "I was so worried about you. OMG, you look so beautiful." Her neighbor came over, and she added, "This is Sharon. I told you." After silence and a head twist. "Isn't she beautiful?"

Penny did her full-body tail wag, circling through my legs and adjusting to her new surroundings. We both squinted as we adjusted to the light.

That was the first time in my entire life I had heard my mother say that I was beautiful. Or anything remotely like that. My holding back tears wasn't necessary, because I was in shock and partly dissociated. Completely numb from the past few years of the insidious destruction of my psyche and loss of any ideal I'd had about my life existing somewhere else.

I had some money left over from my trip. I went through my things, including my jewelry box, and I hawked whatever valuables I had left. Nothing was going to get in the way of my healing.

Toward the end of our marriage, Andy and I had had to go to a pawn shop to sell what we could, to pay to live. He was fired from every job he got (though it was never his fault, according to him). I had already sold most of my estate and jewelry, but I did have a few things left, like my wedding rings and gifts from him.

I was determined to do everything and anything I could to heal. I wanted to understand what was within me that had led me to be unable to comprehend or see who he truly was. What was within me that initially said yes? No matter how many times I tried to leave, I always went back. I later learned that, with interpersonal violence, the victim leaves and goes back to the abuser an average of nine times. I think my count was at five. That was enough. Now, nothing was going to stop me from understanding who I truly was. The weight of this pain created the inverse energy to propel me forward.

As mentioned earlier in this chapter, we may try to create our own laws, but the universal law of metaphysics shows us we can attempt to defy quantum metaphysics, and the outcome may continue to keep you in a loop of negative outcomes. We know that flight is not possible without weight. The weight of the container has to be equivalent to the metaphysical energy lifting it. This energy responds to what is inside of you as much as what goes on around you. Thrust must be present for forward motion but is not possible without a drag or pull. You can use the heaviness of your truth and of the collective truth that exists to propel you forward.

I had plenty of things in my life that were heavy and that actively and intentionally tried to hold me down and back. It is the existence of these things that helped me to create my own flight school. Throughout my life as an international healer, performance coach, and therapist, I have taught many other dragons and warriors how to fly.

Today, I had a two-hour FaceTime session with my therapist, since the four-hour round trip without traffic didn't fit in my schedule this week. My therapist looked at me through the screen and said, "You are lucky to be alive."

It had taken weeks of double sessions with her for me to share my full journey: what had happened, all that I had left. I found her on social media after following her posts on domestic violence and abuse. I'd messaged her while I was on my trek north after leaving Andy and said, "I think I need your help." Within days, we'd had our first session, and during it she made me promise not to go back. One day at a time, I promised myself and her to not go back.

One of the bravest things you can do is to ask for help. Life is not meant to be a proving ground for how strong you are and how much you can take. Asking for help saved my life.

"I've learned not to measure my strength by how much pain I can endure. I now measure it by the number of things I can let go and replace the empty space with love"

—SJL

Today, my therapist came on full-force. I was ready, and her timing was perfect. Until that point, I hadn't registered that this was all about me. That I was married to a sociopath. A wolf in sheep's clothing. The depths of his illness were tragically deep, so much so that he fooled many of us. It took two months to empty enough of the brainwashing and truth-seeking to see clearly. I had been an easy target and was intentionally targeted. I wrote:

The dance of the narcissist

The loneliness and loss in loving you. What was meant to set free and a breath of fresh air turned into suffering no one should bear.

Kind words carefully spoken, as though you see my soul while studying mine, using its knowledge to catch others in your net. A black hole of fearful need angrily unmet.

My heart reached to yours or was it projection? My own light and your armor created a reflection. Too late to turn around. My fatal flaw. I yearned to heal the deepest of wounds. The need to be needed. Lifetimes of misguided teachings showing their duality.

Unaware of your identity, a master chameleon, confusion and chaos are your shield. Wolf in sheep's clothing, luring, casting a trance long enough to sink your teeth deep into my skin.

I recall being this scared once when I was nine. A nightmare of a man dressed in a trench coat, neck covered in fur, an animal's head propped on his shoulder. Pure death smoldering in his beady little eyes. He tried to kill me in that dream. With a butcher's knife. Night after night, over and over, I'd scream.

But now, here you are, with all your demons showing. Somehow, I can't scream. Fixing my eyes, I look into you. Shrugging my shoulders, I think. Did you think no one would see? Is this the tragedy? Or is it me?

Your broken bits kept sharp, just like in my dream. Each tip a precise point ready to slice, cloaked beneath your coat. Smiling sabers shine as they sneak a peek.

Is this to scare me away or lure me in? Not much time to think.

You called me your queen. Know I'll never wear your crown. I now see your filthy darkness swimming in oceans meant to drown.

Blessings from above, though a gift I'd never give. The strength from this lesson is learning how to live. Fear has no place in a heart meant to set free thousands of others ready to BE.

We've all banded together from the likes of you now. Higher powers of LOVE, connection, service, and peace are our passion. Our guide. We've taken the poison you spew and swallow it whole. Chase it back with your flames, and lick our lips clean. We powerful beings stride forward with purpose, knowing our loving family rises together. Just. Like. My. Dream.

Awakened mystics, ready, create the antidote to save others lying lifeless over a pew. We healers must heal. Just as our ancestors did, the job is never done.

One last thing that must be said. For this is MY truth. It's. My. Turn. To. Speak.

I believe in miracles, the infinite, the divine (or I would be dead). There is not one ounce of hatred I will allow in my heart. Your darkness is yours to heal. For this, I love and forgive you for all that's been done to create the demons you keep as tenants in your own head.

Today, the severity of this danger hit me. The number of times I was in the car when he tried to run another car off the road, throwing things at the windshield of another driver on the highway, instigating fights with strangers;

the paranoid aggression, the gun and its many appearances, the manipulation, the love bombing, the lies, and all the secrets that were kept—the amount was beyond baffling.

Something else also landed that never had before. I left on July 19. It was now December 1 and the first time it had sunk in that no one in my family acknowledged that I had been the one to experience this abuse and trauma, except my therapist. Not my parents, aunts, uncles, or cousins. They literally didn't connect. Not a word or not affirming anything.

My therapist was the only one. That someone cared for me in this way opened up the floodgates, from which flowed an epiphany that I was not at fault for my programmed beliefs and the ways I saw myself. I was carrying around a metaphorical lamp, looking for the energy source to plug into. Today was the day it all connected, and I saw the light. It illuminated everything.

I sat in a lump on the floor in the closet of my mother's house, where I was staying because I had fled from a toxic marriage. I had left all my belongings behind save my children's artwork, my important documents, clothes, and photos of my daughters. I saw all of it flash and gash as I purged the sooty darkness from inside my body.

From my heart.

From my soul. I emptied. The same way I had learned to after my stroke. 2004 was the closest I had been to my intuition since childhood. I'd followed my inner guidance to find my way out. I always knew that Western medicine didn't always work; it most definitely didn't see the whole person or understand the energetics of trauma, disease, and true healing. I committed myself to becoming less. I surrendered in a freefall from my tree of illusion.

For the first time in my life, I let everything go. I cried, moaned, heaved, and fought the contractions as the spirit of what *was* exited in waves.

Holy shit! It was not my fault for becoming a people-pleaser, an avoidant person who feared intimacy with anyone. It was not my fault for the countless men who took advantage of me for the benefit of their ego and their own darkness. That somewhere along the way to my being born I had been programmed that I was unwanted, hard to love, too sensitive, too much, too out there, and that I then chose the person who would never be able to love me or provide me with the safety and protection of a sacred relationship. My husbands were both not wired to see and live in truth. Therefore, love was an illusion manufactured by each other's wounds. Religion perpetuated this. My whole life, I was shamed into believing I was to blame. Trauma is tricky like that. Shame is also our guide to healing.

I had come to understand that people who have unhealed trauma seek information. Our nervous systems "know" there is a bad guy out there. Something out of place and a threat. If this threat isn't easily visible, we do one of a few things: we make something up in our minds or interrogate others to solve the mystery that we think exists.

These can be handy tools for our survival in the right circumstances. Those whose tools of survival become part of their personality have an infinite number of hooks to keep us on the line. We think we can't escape. I thought I only had one choice to escape the abuse, which was to guard my heart with a bitter self-loathing and never-ending loop of letting someone with a disordered and warped lens determine the value of my worth.

I realized that my mother, who is the chief interrogator and my primary abuser, showed me the greatest contempt and abandonment. She was also the only one who showed up when I had no other place to go. The traumatic bonding had persisted across my entire life. And hers. And my father's. And their parents'. And so on.

I also became aware of the fact that I had abandoned anything within me that was remotely like her.

I started a list of the things I saw in her. I flashed back to sitting poolside with my kindergarten friends, Jamie, Cyn Russell, and my sister, preparing for swim lessons or the dance lessons with the bumble bees or the many rides in the bumpy car to riding lessons and weekends at the place that consistently saved my life, that barn with the mystical dragons who had taught me how to work with my gifts.

It was my mother who, despite her bitterness and toxic relationship with my father, did make the effort to place me in places where I could grow.

She showed me strength.

She showed me determination.

She showed me ignorance.

She showed me the complexities of abuse.

She showed me what unhealed trauma looks and feels like.

My father

He showed me the essence of timing.

He showed me the evidence of resilience.

He showed me how to keep going despite challenges.

He showed me how to think independently.

He showed me how to be sensitive to others with disabilities.

He showed me how to control my emotions.

He showed me that men can weep.

He showed me that hiding hurts.

And I started the journey to forgive the source of my greatest wounding. I asked for forgiveness, to forgive, and to be forgiven. And as I surfaced from the closet, she broke in to interrogate me. She had been listening and her paranoia had taken hold.

I stared through my mother, lost in another dimension, until I was snapped back by her saying, "Don't you dare look at me with that ugly face. It's disgusting. I'm asking you who you were talking to. Was it *him? Does he know where *my granddaughters* are?" She pointed her finger directly at my face to punctuate every word. "*Huh?* Because if he comes anywhere near them, I'll kill him." Her finger closing in on my face, she added, "I. *Will. Kill. Him!* What he did to them is *unforgivable.*"

Even in this moment, she could not acknowledge my existence in the experience.

A short loop of pain and suffering for another's lack of effort to forgive themselves and their past becomes one's constant.

Because I didn't understand the hooks that sink into the spine/the physical representation of eternal life force, the existence of their spirit in their experiences kept me stuck in their suffering. I was programmed to believe I was responsible for others' pain. For hers, my father's, Tom's, Andy's.

I was never good enough for them to choose to get better. I was never truly seen and present in their lives. So, I did everything I could to serve more, perform more, sacrifice more, try more, save more, and work more. I was shredded to a thin piece of string, following it along down a one-way street going the wrong way. I forgave myself for not knowing. I forgave myself for all of the misguided choices I made in this lifetime.

The positive effects of forgiveness are real-life magic. Once you experience the freedom of finding your own forgiveness, you can no longer "not see" truth at its more organic place. The beautiful mystic Prakasaka teaches the meaning of voodoo. It is French for "spiritual atom." Neither can be seen, but we know both exist. His teachings show us that, once we understand we all have access to this, we all have access to universal God.

No matter how misguided, we all have access to universal God. It was my time to look even further inward and create the practice that deconstructed anything that was not in alignment with my soul's truth.

———————•◦●◗◖●◦•———————

Chapter Nine

The Practice of Preparation

My silence was my spiritual warfare.
Spiritual cleansing became my ritual
Physical fitness and health my fight
And forgiveness my alchemy.

I went into a voluntary vipassana or silence. I stopped any conversation with Andy, I stopped feeding my mother's fears with information. I stopped thinking about my father and the last time we'd spoken, months prior, and wondering why he didn't call to check on me, why didn't he defend me when my mother turned my admissions of abuse by my neighbor into an oration about herself. I turned my eyes upward and visualized being in my own sacred space. It became the call of my inner spiritual warrior. My greatest connection to spirit was found in sitting in silence.

I studied the goddess Kali Durga and visualized taking the darkness spewed toward me and eating it as my fuel. I transmuted it into my own passionate determination to move forward to my true destined purpose. I did two hours of NAAM yoga and mantra as taught by Guru Naam Dr. Joseph Michael Levry. I meditated while chanting to the Goddess of abundance Lakshmi and visualized calling in each and every one of my new clients. I found a J.O.B., to support myself as I built my business back from zero.

A month later, I found my launch pad. A tiny apartment in a cute little one-horse town. I named it my "launch pad."

My mother was on another international vacation. I informed her I wouldn't be in her home anymore when she returned. I ignored the barrage of fearful interrogations just as I did when I'd started my master's program the month prior.

"How are you going to do that? Go to school full time and work full time? You're too old to have student loans. I don't know how you can afford to live. What if you don't get a job as a therapist when you're finished? The pay is terrible...."

My response was, "Then I'll do something else. I'll adapt. I'll grow from the experience. I'll succeed no matter what." My words and actions said, "Watch me." My soul said, "I *know* who I am and my purpose. I am just clearing the way to serve."

I intuitively followed what was best for me.

I woke at 5:30 every morning and dressed in layers for my run. No matter the weather, I put feet to ground and ran. I returned to shower, do my mantras, yoga flow, and journaling, to visualize and call in my ascension and abundance. I knew who I was now, and I knew my calling. Then. I'd sit in complete silence. Go to work, do sessions afterward, review my day before I went to bed, and sleep for at least eight hours. Every day.

I came to realize God's message to get strong was sprinkled throughout my whole life. I'd had a tremendous amount of practice carrying everyone else's heaviness. We popularized this idea by naming it "being empathic." I don't believe this is true. I realize now it was the Universe's way to help me gain strength where I was weak.

Anyone who has experienced childhood trauma, especially in younger lifespan development, knows how long they can go without their basic needs being met. They also know how to read someone else's energy. When the two intersect, this breeds entanglement, not empathy.

I had spent much of my energy healing an infinite amount of disease: Epstein Barr, PCOS, fibromyalgia, migraines, celiac, stroke, infertility, insulin resistance, high blood pressure, chronic infection, depression, anxiety, all of which were caused by false programming and perpetuated by a system designed for me to be sick, while uninformed about the truth of the effects of trauma.

Now, I couldn't unsee what I knew as divine truth. I had stopped the momentum from the old waves of normalcy as much as I could, so I could heal. Trying to heal a wound while you pick the scab is near to impossible. I discerned the difference and now the heavy lifting was for me to be a pure channel and vessel. For *me*, because I am. No other reason necessary. But I also knew that, although many times in my life I felt out of place, I was always in the right place as a child of the universe, I was also gifted as the mother of two beautiful and gifted daughters. I also learned that I get to choose where I place people and how I exchange energy with them. It doesn't matter "who" they are to you. This may be simple for some, but not for a child of perpetuated ancestral trauma. Family loyalty is a much-misinterpreted ideology.

It is not until you can drink from your own cup that you experience the magic of your own elixir.

One of the greatest practices was when I learned to experience my own gifts. To turn my healing hands toward my own body, mind and soul. It is not until you can drink from your own cup that you experience the magic of your own elixir. Your magic. Your presence. Your gift to the world is knowing your own medicine. With utmost humility and compassion, that became my daily practice.

It is only then that you understand your worth and the worthiness of equitable energy exchange. It is best always to remember your worth. You are always and forever worthy and just enough for everything and all.

———————•••••———————

The sun broke through a crack in the window blinds, nudging me to wake. Crimson leaves waved me on as I tossed back the sheets.

I had named my apartment "The launch pad." I resisted putting any furniture in it other than a bed, two chairs, a table, and mirrors. The permanence of anything that held me down was anxiety-provoking. I wanted to be untethered in every way. Though it had been months since

I left Andy, I was still afraid he'd find me. I was still ready to run.

Leaving space in my home and having few material possessions felt safe, free, and full of possibilities.

A ray of sun illuminated my yoga mat, welcoming me to my morning ritual. The scent of rose incense tickled my nose as I sat cross-legged, eyes closed, feeling the light of day touch my skin.

Being present with my body, swaying, humming, and smiling, my movements became larger. Seeking the hum of the universe, I moved through sun salutations, staying extra-long in the asanas that felt like a yes, and being gentle while I found my edge in any challenging asanas.

I give myself permission to move and raise my hips to open my sacral chakra. The womb—the place of receiving, the place of abundance, the place where the magic of connection creates. It was the place I had abandoned decades earlier. Once an artist, I became mute to all mediums. I practiced exploring the places that hurt and releasing the spots that resisted. An energetic bubble broke loose from my labrum and boiled up through my spine, exiting from my throat.

I've learned to enjoy the fascinating process of being a witness to our tri-phased existence. The intersection of our bodies, our minds, and our higher power. The heat of the ball in my throat burned until a well of tears fell.

My younger self was fully present and ready to be seen and held. I allowed her to speak, to communicate in our original tongue, telepathically. She finally felt safe to share how hard it was to raise herself. To protect herself when she wanted what was natural, to be considered worthy of protection, nurturing, and safety by the ones who chose to bring her into this world. She saw all along that she was treated differently and now knows what could have been, had she not been the subject of others' bitterness and suffering.

Grief washed over us both as we mourned what could have been, had I understood my own presence. I let the grief run through me and felt its sharp stabbing until it didn't.

Wiping the tears across my mat, I sat again. Visualizing my client family, my children, my new communities, I magnified how wonderful it felt to help others discover how healthy love and total health could be. Healing the impossible, healing my fellow healers of the world dressed up as doctors, athletes, financial geniuses, entrepreneurs, singers, poets, and actors, all learning what an incredible gift they are and how much they are needed to be in their full expression in this world.

I dressed in layers for my run and set off on the road. I could see my breath from the cold. My cadence kicked in quickly, every stride pushing off with a relaxed, powerful force. Somehow, it made me long to ride a horse again. I was ready to feel that connectedness again.

A voice came through and I thought about how I had evaded my alchemy most of my life, because I hadn't realized the personal responsibility in my experience. I was so deeply programmed and dissociated from myself that I misunderstood the powerful impact I made on others. Good or not so good. I first had to deconstruct the false truth of my original experience, in order to understand my responsibility. I acknowledged my responsibility for having caused wrong and forgave the catalyst to my conflicts.

I was now ready to peel back the layers while I continually sought forgiveness and love, and finally to express gratitude for every single bit of it. No matter how brutal the truth. Let it be found with grace. I remember my therapist saying that one-dimensional is boring. I bristled at this, at first. Now, I fully understood and agreed that we are best when we are present fully in our multifaceted selves and used this as my platform to serve high performers. Why work to niche down when we are meant to expand and express *all* of ourselves?

Ho'oponopono

"I'm sorry. Please forgive me. Thank you. I love you."

These simple words of ancient Hawaiian wisdom, their traditional practice of reconciliation and forgiveness, have a powerful effect.

I was ready to forgive myself for hurting my children. I forgave myself for failing. I asked for forgiveness every day and told everyone I loved them. I still do to this day.

In the beginning, it brought a visceral effect.

In a run in the dead of winter, I was miserable. I thought I had left New Jersey winters behind. Taking a full stride forward, my body collapsed like a Swiss Army knife. It folded over, and my stomach hurled a ball of sticky tar. It came as a projectile from my mouth.

My eyes were half shut and I found myself by a tree. Leaning against it, my knees buckled. With every contraction from my gut, I'd buckle, thinking each time, "I don't want to fall off the side of this snowy trail."

I held on to that tree for literal dear life as I was tossing and releasing and crying with every pass. I'd catch my breath and say, "I'm sorry, please forgive me, I forgive you, I love you."

Visions of my daughters' traumatized faces flashed, and I let myself feel the pain repeating, "I'm sorry, I love you, I hope you forgive me," and I continued with my vow to never let that happen again.

My younger self, all of my younger me, looked on with wife eyes as I said, "Thank you for doing your best to take care of me. I am sorry. I will protect you. I will listen to you. I will give you what you need, no matter what or when. I hope you forgive me."

Know this ultimate and endless divine truth of the beginning of the beginning of your ancestors. It is what they have always given us, ours to freely see. Love thrives between truth and embodied wisdom of your unique experiences.

I remembered the nights when my sister and I were out exploring the apple orchard in my neighborhood as children. We were called home for dinner by my mother ringing the bell.

I recalled the time I saw my mother angrily defending me from the neighborhood bully, who tormented me for years.

I remembered my sister rising up like a lioness, pinning the same bulky boy on the ground for trying to push me down into the grass on a pile of dog poop, then holding dog poop on the end of a stick and poking it into his face, screaming, *"Leave my sister alone!"*

I remembered being thirteen and seeing my father weep at a concert in the park as he sung, full voice, along with the performers on stage, knowing that he, too, wished to be on stage, performing. Weeping to live a life in greater expression.

I remembered, years after my divorce and Tom's continued divisive abuse, being the only one to drive two hours in a snow storm because my children called to tell me their father, who had a TBI and spinal injuries, had slipped on the ice and hit his head, and he had amnesia. I walked into the ER room to find him completely incapacitated and unable to recognize anyone.

I worked with him to remind him that I was the mother of his children and his friend for most of our lives. He introduced me as his wife to the doctors and let me tell them everything they needed to know. Healing does that. Living your purpose raises you above all chaos and allows you to live, serve, and love.

I am grateful to my mother for the opportunity to have a place to stay after I fled from my second marriage.

I am grateful for my mother's strength, my father's leaving, and my sister's loyalty to the family.

I have infinite gratitude for my grandparents, who gave up so much of their lives to serve their family and future generations.

I had to understand how affected I was by the trauma of my life in order to understand that I needed to forgive myself and others. Without truth, it is impossible to embody the wisdom of our transformation. Or to have an appreciation for how incredible I really am. To know how incredible we all are!

With every step toward forgiveness, I felt more compassion for others. I organically felt more love for myself. For all of my younger selves.

Practicing forgiveness is simple in its steps and challenging in its content, especially if you are the victim of insidious abuse. In that case, try forgiving yourself. Think of something that is weighing you down, and try these easy steps.

Step One: "I'M SORRY"

Step 2: Ask Forgiveness – "PLEASE FORGIVE ME"

Step 3: Gratitude – "THANK YOU"

Step 4: Love – "I LOVE YOU"

CHAPTER TEN

THE HEALERS JOURNEY

You own everything that happened for you. To release your stifled voice, tell the stories of your healing.

There is a notion that many are on the precipice, in or on a spiritual awakening. While I agree, I want to expand this to the awakening of our individual and collective healing. Everything and anything can be healed, transformed, changed, and transmuted through the understanding and experience of the spirit/spirituality. Without this, we are only as traveled as our finite brains will allow.

There are no coincidences, between the rise of a global epidemic (anxiety and fear) of disease and the birth of new disorders and mutations of disease from a historical perspective and the increase of individual crises and a sign on the wall that says "You can't continue until you unpack your conflicts." Your disease.

It is also no coincidence that part of our spiritual and metaphysical ascension involves physical sensations, symptoms such as fever, fatigue, and autoimmune diseases, and emotional and psychological disturbances or distress. Psychiatrist and thought pioneer Carl Jung popularized the concept of an *awakening*. This is usually brought upon by a life-altering event. These events ask us to rise into a higher state of consciousness, not intelligence.

The most common thing to bring about an awakening is trauma. There are parallel descriptions made between scientific, spiritual, and psychological communities and practitioners that say the same thing in different language. Events plant the seed of change.

Many things that come from the awakening increase your inherent gifts. Your sensitivities. But I believe we need to expand this context and awareness further. To see how the impact of our awakening was important, but, much like our own growth, that it isn't the end.

Our awakenings prepare us for the next greatest job of all: to break generational cycles and learn how to heal our own inner conflicts, so we create the compassion to help one another to heal.

It's time to shift our focus from seeking a cure to healing to be well.

Medicine cures what is presenting as the biggest threat or problem. We seek to find cures for cancer, heart disease, autoimmune diseases like fibromyalgia, irritable bowel, paralysis, chronic pain, Epstein Barr Syndrome, and so on, but it really doesn't *heal why it surfaced*. In my practice, many people come to me with the most "treatment-resistant" disease and a laundry list of medications and specialists who are treating the disease.

But what if I asked you if you wanted to *heal* whatever it was that was in conflict that was manifesting itself as disease?

"A healthy immune system can defeat invading disease-causing germs (or pathogens), such as bacteria, viruses, parasites—as well as cancer cells—while protecting healthy tissue."

—Pfizer, Inc.

What is in the way of a healthy system? Conflict. A lack of agreement between the body, mind, spirit, and its environment. The beautiful part about healing is you need not know exactly how, but you need to start by becoming a master of yourself. From there, you can help others be a better expression of themselves.

A friend recently told me a story about a consultant. He was in charge of recruiting and placement of talent. He asked her what she wanted to do, and as she answered he "read" her energy.

He said, "I was with you until you said... You don't really want to do that, do you?"

She laughed and said, honestly, no. "But not for reasons you think..."

From there, the conversation went from two people doing their job to their connecting and aligning with each other's truth.

When she told me he'd told her he was a medium, I said that made sense. "He likes to use his gifts to help make the deal happen successfully." He knows his gifts, and he uses them in his work to serve well.

The thing is, you may not have known about your gifts or superpowers when you were born. Or maybe, like me, you had early (womb) trauma that awakened sensitivity before birth. Maybe, like me, you were born directly into the center of a kaleidoscope. A full-on spectrum of visions, knowing, sensations, smells, sounds, and communication beyond words. The polarizing effect of living in the stillness, darkness, and confinement of a dissociated state from a troubled womb to being born into the bright rainbow of light and energetic and vibrational downloads in one or all of your senses can be overwhelming. Paralyzing.

No matter when it comes through, be sure to listen to your calling.

There is a whisper happening that you can't consciously hear. It is telling you to live your life as big as you can, so that you experience your ultimate Heaven on Earth. It's your Healer's Journey.

I have noticed an increase in the number of empaths, highly sensitive persons, and neurodivergent. I believe this is the first predisposition we need in order to understand all aspects of life historically, so we can prepare for a new age of life for this planet and beyond. The dark and the light and all it represents are an affirmation that we are here and we are whole.

The rise of epidemics like anxieties, depression, and addiction also are the result of the magnified nature of the above. Imagine living life in full technicolor in all ways, all the time. Part of our ancestral heritage is that we have all, as a collective, been born to generations of survival. Most of our ancestors lived with a heightened sympathetic nervous system response all the time.

Epigenetic studies show us that unhealed trauma from ancestors whom we have never met or seen or touched exists in our bodies. These traumas have severed us in many positive ways, as well as in hardship, and have seen and unseen wounding. All indicators point to a more evolved human being, if we seek to heal.

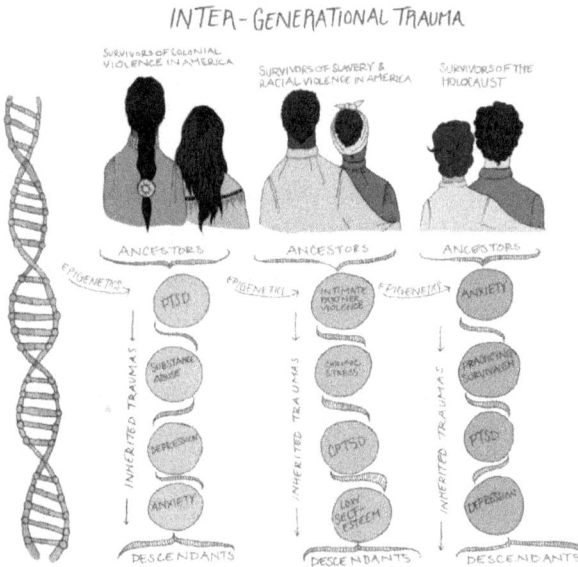

Epigenetic factors show that inherited trauma from past generations is scientifically evident

Intergenerational trauma presents differently for different generational descendants. Europeans who survived the European wars show, through epigenetics, various traumas passed through multiple generations, such as: PTSD, alcoholism, sexual abuse, and emotional repression. Throughout the American South and South Africa, traumas have passed on, including, abandonment, domestic violence, low self-esteem, and CPTSD. British India passed through their generations traumas that include poverty consciousness, suffocating shame based on social rules, severe anxiety, and depression.

When we heal and work through our own trauma, we are helping heal the trauma of our ancestors and for future generations. Narcissistic personality disorder and other personality challenges (cluster B personality disorders) are the potential result of unhealed intergenerational trauma.

But there is another side to your healing and trauma: growth and resilience! The more we heal and grow, the stronger and more resilient we are for any and all collective and individual events. A HSP (highly gifted and sensitive person) is highly tuned to heal past traumas. They are a powerhouse for our future collective healing.

These people are so highly tuned that they are mirrors for what is happening collectively. Their healthy response is the manifestation of disease. The suffering experienced is the denial of their gifts as part of their reality. They are being called on to master themselves as pure, safe, neutral, and healthy, so they can connect with others to experience the same.

Simultaneously, the number of artists, creatives, and expressives is rising. This is despite the cutbacks by our institutions and schools. Trauma increases the ability to access information differently in the brain. Many who have experienced childhood or complex trauma are extremely talented artists.

One of my adolescent clients with South Asian ancestry was riddled with panic attacks, depression, and off-the-charts pain, along with other physical markers of disease. Their prior year had been spent in crisis. They came to me through a referral, and in our first session, I asked what their hopes were from our work together.

"To not be so overwhelmed by the world around me."

They had been through a long list of practitioners, and they were kind but distant in our first sessions. They rarely looked into the camera and always appeared to be doing "something." I was fine with this, considering they were fully engaged in our talks. Just not looking at me.

When I checked in with them a few sessions in, I asked if they felt they were being served well. "Are you happy with our healing and therapeutic relationship?"

Looking directly at the video, they said, "You are the first person who listens to me, respects me, and validates my experiences. Yes. Yes, I am benefiting from our sessions, and it's the only reason why I try the things you ask me to do in between sessions. You have seen me in ways others can't or won't."

Without context of common practice in a culture, we can be significantly traumatized by those offering to help.

In a monotone voice, they uttered, "The rules of many affect the rules of one."

I looked through the video and said, "I appreciate you so much. You are strong and compassionate to choose to see and be in a world that has overwhelmed you. We humans set up so many rules, which are an attempt to keep us safe but only in the context of our environment. When you are a child of the universe, it can temporarily feel like it keeps us from living free. Or it can be extremely shocking to our nervous system. But part of this journey is to learn how to exist in harmony with all. To live with a coherent heart and mind and to embrace our wild. Your own version of expression.

"You already know about the infinite. It's part of your job now to understand finite thinking. It will give you the wisdom you need. Maybe your journey right now is to understand how to turn limited into unlimited, so you can feel a sense of ease and freedom. Maybe then you can share your gifts with the world, just like the animals you speak of."

Western medicine addresses a person like this by presenting a cure, like medications for anxiety, depression, plus a sprinkle of medication to sleep and mood stabilization. None of these address the healing that this beautiful soul is here to experience for himself and for his ancestors and our world.

His mother called me to thank me for not giving up on him. Sobbing, she said, "I know my child, and they needed someone to not give up, because they have trouble with systems and change. This exact relationship and work, to help them through this difficult time. Thank you for meeting them with an open mind and heart. They are a very gifted child." She agreed to support any testing and energy work needed to help get to the root causes to heal. She admitted this was a generational experience, and she worried in hindsight that would affect them more by moving to the US.

As an HSP (highly gifted and sensitive person), had I not gone through my own struggles with this and also had the experience with countless others, I would not have had the confidence to go outside the lines drawn to provide them with what they needed. Healing is an unfolding of health, awareness, emptying, and transmutation of what is in conflict to harmony. This pain of what is is directed by the wound; it is healed by loving and feeling grateful for it, not by a cauterizing or cutting the wound.

Like many of my cases, I have worked with several members within the family. Mothers, fathers, grandparents, children, husbands, wives, and "victim and perpetrators." I came to realize through my own healing that we have a powerful effect on systems, inter-generational trauma, and epigenetics (discussed earlier), if we all work to heal in tandem. I expand the lens to work with any and all individuals in multiple generations. When we heal, we create spaces for others to heal. It is profound.

I was asked to perform a husband-and-wife healing in 2019, after the wife had a traumatic miscarriage. She had invested in any and all to understand "why" and how to plan for her next, so this didn't happen again. She wanted a full report on dates, etc., that would guarantee her a healthy child. I, in the other hand, was guided to tell her about her own alignment, her own ways to heal, and I gave her very specific insight into her health body, mind, and soul. I visited their home and gave both her and her husband a somatic and harmonium healing (as taught by Dr. Levry).

She wasn't sure how to explain the session to her husband, so she said, "It will be relaxing, and you don't have to talk."

He was in.

In hers, we released much lifetime trauma and ancestral trauma. Afterward, she was without words.

Her husband entered in, saying, "Happy wife, happy life," and we all laughed as he looked at her with concern. She had tears in her eyes. The sense of full release that had occurred is indescribable.

During our healing work, the light that flows through your body is fully visible. I don't think he'd seen her in such a sacred state before, and he wondered in part what I'd done to her, and also if I was going to do *that* to him. He tried not to look scared, which set us all into more laughter.

We laughed at the multiple layers of humor, and I secretly knew that that, in itself, was breaking the intersection of their own karma. I could clearly feel the root cause of distress.

As she left, he lay awkwardly on the table. I gave him the broad-strokes introduction around what was going to happen, non-woo-woo husband edition, and we began. At first, he was chatty, and I obliged, until I felt the download begin.

I began to sweat, and my hands were on fire. He began to vibrate as I was solidly the instrument, a witness to his beautiful healing. The bandwidth on this one was large. The trauma released from his spine was plentiful, and with each passing over his heart, it responded and received the light openly. When we finished, much like his wife, he looked peaceful and renewed.

As he poured himself into his office chair, he asked, "What was that?" He was curious and asked fantastic questions, which I answered honestly.

His wife returned, and I said my goodbye.

The following day, I received an email from that client saying they had stayed up most of the night and had the most amazing talk together night. In short, it had saved their marriage. Less than a year later, they had their second child and, with effort, their relationship became a full partnership with equitable love and respect.

In quantum metaphysics, we understand that we are all connected. All parts of the self are interrelated and mirror this to the universe.

We are connected to the love of others, especially those to whom we (on a different timeline) are already connected. When we choose to take positive steps toward our highest self and vibration, it positively affects the one to whom we are "attached" in the quantum. Therefore, our light, our life, and our healing helps others to heal.

The part that most people aren't able to move part is needing to see proof of this, prior to trying. Or, once they've tried, if there is no tangible evidence, they give up. Or they don't believe anything positive has occurred. This explains why some of us get and stay stuck.

Generational healing usually initiates because someone is struggling emotionally or physically or both. We start our transformative work, and as they change and become a glowing beam of light and health, other family members want to heal, too. It's a beautiful unfolding of the universe's natural order.

As I was writing this final chapter, another family whom I've worked with in the prismatic container came into focus. So far, they have two adult children and the father in the prismatic container. I received a text message. It was from the mother, who had initiated the referral for her family. She said she had to tell me that, on Christmas Day, seated at the family table, they went down the line to ask what each one was grateful for. The son replied, "I am grateful for Sharon, because she helped me change my life."

I will never take for granted the work I get to do every single day. It isn't always easy, but it is always worth it. Because of my own determination and healing, the door was opened for me to help others.

I still believe in the power of the multiverse and metaphysics. I realize that everyone who presents themselves to me, asking for help, allows me to go deeper into myself and seek a higher state of health.

I thought back to a pivotal moment between my own mother and me, years ago.

Looking at me like I had completely lost my mind (per usual), she was anxiously discussing my daughter, Lizzy, who was struggling with school and life. It was during the time when Lizzy had completely blocked me from her life. I later learned that her father had capitalized on the situation and manipulated, gaslit, and lied to anyone he could, to build a case to divide her and me. Yes, she had gone through a traumatic experience, and I was doing everything I could to get her the help she needed—

therapy, healing, resources, and family. But she and he resisted and eventually sabotaged all of it.

I understood the ancestral trauma and karma she was working through, in part because I was doing it, too. As proof of the generational gesture, my mother yelled, "What are you going to do about this? Are you going to set Tom straight? Call the principle? Write the superintendent?"

I breathed deep belly breaths and said, "No, Mom, I'm going to heal. To work on myself. It's the only thing I have control over, and it's the only thing that will give her a chance to get better."

As she slammed her things down on the table, I walked away, formulating a plan to carve out the time I needed to do this work.

The neurosis and constant worry and anxiety was crippling my daughter, much like the energy presented by my mother. If either of them had any chance to transmute to a greater extent of health, I had to find it by healing anything that resembled that within me.

Already in therapy, I started to ask around to see what else was available. I learned a global healing with a spiritual teacher was happening the next day. Over eleven thousand others and I signed up to connect together.

I had no idea that I would be actively doing movement, mantra, and sound vibration for three hours. It felt incredible. It was exactly what I was missing: intentional connection with others like myself. In the days that followed, I increased my running, mantra, sound vibration, meditation, and Naam yoga, as taught by Dr. Levry.

I was also determined to become a better mother. On my runs, I visualized how it would feel to be in a healthy relationship with both of my girls. I saw us together, not as it was, not as I was told by family and society it was supposed to be, but as it was *meant to be,* with both of them healing themselves and others.

At times, I folded over onto a tree on the trail in full release. I'd have flashbacks to moments when I knew my activation and survival had hurt them. Facing this truth was no easy task. It was hard to accept what this starting point was for all of us. I was anxious about my future (I'd lost everything I had), but I fought my own worry with trust.

Each time, I had to confront my situation, because people would know but not say. Shame would try to take hold. Instead, I let it serve as my humility and motivation to carry on. One foot in front of the other, I was building a life that I wanted to live, instead of just survive.

I adapted the Acronym triple-A:

* ✳ *Awareness*
* ✳ *Acceptance*
* ✳ *Action*

Even though I was decades into my healing journey, after having my first major uprooting in 2004, I was unaware of the fact that I had continued to re-pattern toxic and abusive relationships in my life. Once I became aware of this, I had to accept my responsibilities in each situation. When I drove over 1,000 miles away from the life I knew, I was faced with the question: "What do I need to heal in order to *never* be in that situation again?" This allowed me to heal the lens through which I viewed myself and life. Once healing began, I took action in co-creating a life that was in alignment with who I truly am.

Applying these principles to each new venture and old experience guided me to my next right step. It created clarity to see and to fully accept all of who I am and am meant to be, in this lifetime.

You must see yourself as the soul who was hurt and address each one, to set them free, in order for you to be free.

Most of my life, it wasn't safe to be who I truly was. I learned I have been in fight-or-flight mode for most of my life. I had to understand what it did to my brain and my body. In the absence of my abusers, I continued to surround myself with people who weren't safe. They weren't able to see me. I had to heal what was within me that was afraid to be seen, and to connect and to share in equal energy.

I used to be selective with whom I shared definitively the multi-spectrum ways I communicate and receive information. But if I expected anyone to see, embrace, use, and love their gifts, then I had to see, embrace, use, and love mine.

In my case, my traumatic childhood, which included narcissistic abuse, sexual assault and torture, psychological abuse and torture, lack of emotional and physical safety, and the laundry list of autoimmune diseases and physical crises that showed up, helped to keep the wound open. Like a flashing neon sign saying, *"Follow me here!"* My psychic and otherworldly gifts were the cause of many of my traumas and, on a different timeline, were the key to set me free into full expression.

The more I hid, the more I hurt

It is that simple.

I'm asked all the time to give a how-to on what to address in order to transform. My answer is simple: follow the disease. Listen to the conflict inside of you. Let your discomfort be the neon sign to follow down the spiraling path to your wound. Heal and love everything on the way down. You are not just here to cross a finish line, check a box, or create a list. Rather, you are here to deconstruct what isn't in coherence with the truth. Your truth. And the truth of the ages. Our history.

Part of your own healer's journey is to embrace the karma (lessons) that you are here to learn.

Your journey as a healer is to understand that what you see and what you are shown in this life is exactly what you need to see, so you can create and act on it. You are a "creactive": the perfect blend of masculine and feminine energy; a responder to your growth.

When you are in challenging environments, you are being asked to find ways to help yourself survive. When you are a child in traumatic and challenging environments, you are tasked with growing while you are surviving.

Because this was my experience, I now sense this energetic imprint from blocks away. When I ask my clients what their experience was like as a child, most often I hear, "It was a wonderful childhood. I don't understand why I ended up off course, in a toxic and abusive relationship, addiction, and so on."

Our structured cultural systems, family systems, and religious systems all have a part and say in our beliefs. Most are measured by a simple "good or bad," rather than just the right measure. So, the result is a reward for martyrdom, guilt around abundance, and a sense of hiding from retaliation by the ever-changing and moving goal post to perform, living outside of ourselves.

I perpetuated the rising and falling of elusive abundance because I wasn't operating from the universal law of energy exchange. My identity was lost in making others happy, not in my own soul's expression. Its guidance was stifled by external pressures to be good. The lens I was measuring myself from wasn't mine. I know this now from the responses of my body, mind, and spirit contained within.

It wasn't until I had lost everything that I was given the gift of time and simplicity. I had to stop hiding so I could stop suffering.

I had already learned to do this to myself when I had the first stroke. I sat up for twenty-four hours after leaving the hospital, signing an AMA. Having had the first of many major awakenings in 2004 prepared me for my biggest death. And so, in 2017, I began my greatest birth.

Healers don't have to suffer for others' sake. It's part of what we are all here to do: to help each other learn. My daughters, who are both incredibly talented healers, have taught me that.

I felt grateful.

My daughter Emily looked at me with a distant gaze. This wasn't the homecoming I'd expected, but it was definitely what I needed. She and Elizabeth had intuitively stepped away, so I could face my own fire-breathing dragons. Their bravery to let go was the greatest act of health and love.

Their stepping away broke my heart and soul wide open. To date, that is the most agony I've ever felt. I metaphorically, physically, and spiritually mourned the inability to mother them in the ways I knew how.

We sat in Starbucks, and her big gold-speckled green eyes flitted between my face and her hands. She looked like a model for an advertisement to visit Ireland: pale skin, speckled with freckles across her nose, and long, unruly, wavy brown hair.

With clarity, Emily spoke to her hands. "Mom, I don't want to have the same relationship with you that we had in the past. I don't want you to mother me the way you did. I'm not sure how I want us to be in each other's lives, but I know I don't want to live through this again."

I had to accept the responsibility for my part in their own hurt, something I've never experienced with or from either of my parents in my entire life. I had to trust that she would be okay. My job was to heal whatever I saw within her within me.

It was then that I realized the full capacity of communication with a dragon: not to try to make them anything different or more dangerous, but to love them for their darkness. What I was seeing in front of me with Emily was the hologram of her unhealed darkness, the metabolizing of her painful experience, and the whispering of her soul. All at once. The dragon breathed fire, and I respected its anger and rage. I had to love all of it. All of her, just as I needed to be seen and loved for my life. I was determined to stand strong like a willow in this storm.

We are here to support our children on their journey. To love them and to keep them safe. It is one of the most difficult things in life to say goodbye to your child at every stage they grow through, never knowing who and how they will evolve as they grow. From three to sixty-three, we watch them grow into who they are meant to be. Not who we want them to be.

In my own decades of healing, I worked with shamans, metaphysicians, spiritual masters, and teachers, Buddhist monks, priests, Tibetan healers, doctors, and gurus. I not only learned the keys of outward success, which is our health, body-mind-spirit; I learned the true laws of the universe. To work with mystics in an organic (read non-commodity) way, I was able to study the beginning of the beginning of the word and of Source/God, to use my strength to not be afraid of others' darkness, and use the language needed to trust the divine to work through me.

I learned to never deal directly with another, but to always seek connection with God first, then to whisper into the darkness of others until I could hear in my heart, because I had learned how to see the darkness in mine. Prior to this stage of training, I was programmed to believe I was alone in service. And though I was grateful for my gifts, I thought I had to measure their use myself. I learned how to turn off my own judgement and see through the eyes of the universe. From the astral plane.

Angering to strengthen your boundaries and, reclaiming your own protection is an important part of healing for women, just as grieving and self-compassion is for men, who have both been socialized against their natural and basic needs. (Schwartz, R. 1995).

I also found that our basic needs going unmet during our early lifespan development affects our psychosocial development. Internal Family Systems Therapy addresses the multiple aspects of self along these developmental milestones and allows for our reparenting.

After much of my work with "narcissistic PD," toxic and IPV, and after helping countless high performers, like actresses, professional athletes, creatives, entrepreneurs, and the like, to fully transform their lives by healing the root cause, I had a client call me "The Dragon-Slayer's Whisperer." I reflected that, over the course of my life, I had gone directly into the flames of many of my own and other dragons' fiery roar. Whether it was me, the dragon, or the slayer, I would come as close as I could to whisper, "You find peace for having to become the slayer. In a world of beasts and unruly dragons, it is a noble thing to answer the call."

My mission was to create safe spaces so the coherence and harmony needed to communicate in peace was possible. I knew realistically this was a huge undertaking. It is a daily challenge to reverse the negative voices that say I'm nuts for even trying. *"Who do you think you are?"*

Being surrounded by narcissists prepared me to see this was my own karma. My own personal growth. The lesson my soul needed to learn, in infinite ways.

We are not healed by taking a pill, going on a weekend retreat, reading text, regurgitating information, controlling the mind, or being slick marketers. Narcissistic energy uses this as a means to fill an unsatiated black hole of consumption. We heal by knowing the truth of our highest selves. We heal by understanding the infinite scientific and mathematical calculations of the metaphysical universe.

The fact that our bodies, minds, or level of spirituality show up in disease is a sign of health of the whole. We are taught to believe our healthy response to trauma is abnormal. That is not true. It is abnormal and unhealthy to believe we are to blame for our disease because we are faulty. We live in disease because most of us are hiding behind our own diseases and work harder to maintain our disease than to deconstruct it by any means necessary, to arrive at our pure truth, embodied wisdom, and full capacity of love.

Spirituality and science teach us that each of our organs is their own spirit and is unified with our mind and body. And the spirits of others are interconnected with us through all capacities: mind, energy, bodies, spirit, and soul. We are all connected. So, this directs us to at least consider healing, if not feel compelled to heal, ourselves from deep within, so we can shift the collective bodies, minds, energy, spirits, and souls of all. The great all is within us.

It is from the center of our collective wound that each of you are truly born. We will share in our own way the reflections that catch the light just enough to illuminate what we each carry within. It might show up in different ways, cadence, and timing, some more intensely than others, but all are equally important to attend to.

There is no greater calling for us all right now than to heal. As a mystic, I know this by looking at the Piscean Age we are leaving and the Aquarian Age we have entered. As a human being, I see evidence of this and have lived this. As a visionary, I see this.

If you are reading this, you have had the experience that most ancestors before us have not. You have lived and straddled two different ages. You are experiencing while seeing the intersections of the divine order of change in dramatic and grand-scale ways.

We have all been placed here as instruments, as healers. To heal means to change. Even in your resistance to evolution, you are creating the right conditions for change.

You may not consider yourself religious or spiritual. I'm not here to convince you to choose anything other than what is true for you. The truth is most of us have experienced some level of religious abuse, many in the way we may have experienced trauma in other parts of our lives. In my work with healing from narcissistic, sociopathic, and spiritual abuse, I have learned to utilize pillars of truth as a guide to surrender and live in flow with our energies.

One thing we can agree with is we are here for change.

To evolve = To heal

SHARON LAND

CHAPTER ELEVEN

THE PILLARS OF A HEALER

Being a healer means being the instrument of healing, which comes from a greater collective wisdom and universal source (insert your preferred reference: God, gods, goddesses, Allah, Jesus, universe, source, love). You alone are not the healer. You choose to be the vessel for healing.

A healer is a person who understands and has the insight and practice of self-awareness, not self-deprecation.

They are aware of themselves and their impact on their own selfhood and equally understand the effect of how they impact others.

Healers do not judge their inherent response to their needs and do not judge other people for doing the same.

They do not manipulate other people to serve themselves or to portray a manufactured sense of urgency or need. They do not judge others for choosing what is right for them in that moment.

Healers do not judge others or impose a required level of positivity but rather request transparency.

Healers do not feel entitled to teach others what is right or wrong or feel entitled to forgiveness.

Healers and spiritual people work to understand their own contributions toward enabling, bypassing, or hijacking others' experience, for or providing lessons when not being asked.

Spiritual guidance does not seek to package information in order to provide tickets, consumer packaging, or easy one-two-three guidebooks because they want a fast result for a fast gain.

Healers know the universal law of attraction and exchange. They see how consumerism feeds into an old system that has built its success by denying the full embodiment and expression of truth.

Healers agree to branding but never to create as a brand our highest and best selves or our higher power, only to expand the ability to serve.

Healers recognize narcissistic traits, tendencies, and behaviors as lack of coherence in actions and deeds.

Healers have a daily practice to increase health of spirit, body, mind, and energy. They do not use this as a way to package love, light, and peace to manipulate others to do the same.

Your best blessings, mantra, kriya is to be joyful and healthy and love.

A heart full of peace and joy is the best medicine. Find your way inward, so you can find joy in all circumstances

Let no one define your own health. This includes Western medicine.

I have practiced and experienced the divine in every spiritual teaching and practice.

When you work with and serve other people, you must increase the amount of care for yourself—body, mind, soul.

We must face the falsehood within ourselves, so we can notice the falsehood represented outside of ourselves. Part of this journey is to have a relationship with the side of life that we cannot see.

We have now entered the Aquarian Age. We have had the unique opportunity to live within two different ages. The Piscean Age forced us to be and do alone. The Aquarian Age is asking us to come together.

I choose to not lose sight of this lesson or time. Because I honored the divine and myself, I was given an infinite amount of unimaginable blessings. The steps forward were always illuminated at the perfect time. I dove even deeper into ancient mysticism and studied with shamans and spiritual masters. I traveled the world to be taught by ancient mystics, and I learned the truth of the truth of the true wisdom of the ages.

Though I had access to incredible gifts from birth, I wanted to became an expert, and I was taught to work with the energy we all have access to. I gently, powerfully, and divinely started the process of deconstructing everything I knew to be true. Replacing it with full embodied wisdom.

"Someone I loved once gave me a box full of darkness. It took me years to understand that this was a gift"

—Mary Oliver

By trusting the "signs," I followed the path to my own traumas, the ones I never knew existed. My wounds were my clarity that everything was right with me, including my symptoms and illnesses. Slowly, the wounds became the womb where I gestated, back in the cave once again, on the launch pad that birthed me into full expression. The dichotomy of life is never lost on a healer.

You are a healer. You have been using your gifts on some level all of your life to survive.

Now, it is your calling to rise into a life of collective healing. By resisting the calling to see your inner darkness, you are denying the ability to follow divine order and your personal, customized guide map to your spiritual and causal existence. You are separating yourself from the connection to the infinite, the universe, your highest and best self. You are separating yourself from your ability to serve.

To serve from a place of full coherence of the body, mind, soul, heart, and mind in your own unique fingerprint, you have discovered the key to one of life's mysteries. You have created Heaven on Earth. You are not just a human; rather, you are the breath of the universe exhaling through a physical body and feeding love back into the multiverse.

You. Must. Follow. The. Call.

Trauma is not something we outlive. It is something we face, heal, and transcend.

Sometimes, you just need to detach from everything. In a quest for clarity, realize what binds you, paralyzes you, and what elevates you. Then, do something to improve your alignment with all of it.

I want you to know from a deep, *deep* place within yourself that you are not the one whose opportunity is going to be passed by. You are not alone and never will be alone. You and your suffering are an indication that you are being called up. Called to rise up. Called to lift your eyes, head, and heart up. Called to your highest and best self to rise into peace, ease, and compassion for yourself, your suffering, your life, and our universe. This is and always will be the path of a compassionate healer.

As you rise into your own gifts, no matter where you live or what your profession, reach higher than you believe you can. Your roots are deeply planted into your ancestors' soil. Let the vibrations of your transformation feed intelligence into Mother Earth, so she can continue her own metamorphosis.

Let your mind continue to wander upward, and without judgement, receive the wisdom channeled into you from the universe. This may not make much sense to you in the present moment, but intuition and the unseen of all possibilities rarely does.

See from within the light you reflect, as you continue to expand, express, and grow more into your full self. Take the time to drink from your own cup, taste your own magic, so you can understand the value and worth of all you bring to this world.

When you come to the point of your soul's growth, you realize that you have very little to do with the amount of time you spend in this existence. But it is the way we attend to each moment that matters. The most important part of our essence is the legacy of life we leave behind.

So, whether a coach, accountant, entrepreneur, sound engineer, military, actor, professional athlete, business tycoon, musician, artist, parent, or cook, the way you greet yourself in your own self-growth and work is the way you help others in theirs.

When I say you have greatness inside of you, it means that, no matter the circumstances or feeling or thought you embody, it is your ability to be soft in a moment of pain, where you choose to honor the truth, sacred wisdom, and love, and that you are the instrument being used to transmute this unique experience. It is yours. Whether silently or with a fire-breathing scream, you are shifting the trajectory of your ancestors seven years ahead and back. The winds that blow will shift, the rain that falls will nourish, and a fire that burns will burn brighter because of you.

It is your soul and mind that travel from lifetime to lifetime. Let the wisdom of these experiences become known now. We transcend all things, when we connect to our highest and best selves.

EPILOGUE

She stormed into the therapy room and threw herself in the loveseat with an audible punch. So much so that you could hear the *hissssss* of air escaping the vision. Maybe it, too, was running from the room. This was my first time meeting with her and my first month of being a therapist intern at a busy private practice.

Her face was beet-red, and she rolled up her sleeves as she shouted, "I want you to tell me how to make all of this stop. I can't take it anymore, and I'm sick of all the bullshit. *You* have to tell me right now!"

I sat for a moment in disbelief. I was supposed to be filling in for another therapist. Eager for hours in the chair, I'd said yes, thinking, "How hard can it be?"

The wet-behind-the-ears intern faded and the chief driver of the trauma bus emerged. "Come on in kids! The ride might be bumpy, but we'll make it fun!" Game on. I was keyed in. Dialed in and ready to roll. My entire life had prepared me for this.

"Did you read my file?" Which was, collectively, three binders, each of them six-inches thick.

I almost flinched. For a split second, I thought to lie and say, yes, I had read them. Would this disarm her? Would it make her like me? Then I remembered rule number one of my own life standard: "I say no to suffering."

Instead:

* ✳ Choose presence.
* ✳ Live in the truth of who you are
* ✳ You are just enough
* ✳ and by all means *"don't flinch."*

Healers don't change another's storm. No storm is yours to change. A healer's job is to learn how to weather storms, so they can be a guide for others who are willing to weather theirs well.

Looking directly at her, I couldn't help but smile. I knew I was exactly where I was supposed to be.

———————— •●●◆●●• ————————

When I was approached about writing a book about my life and my experience as a trauma authority and healer, I thought, "How do I write a book about myself when my entire life, my programming has told me that I am invisible?"

I am a classic, card-carrying member of "The Recovering Perfectionist Society," whose trauma response was to perform and be perfect, so I can become visible. With endless amounts of training, certifications, and years of experience working in the healing space, I wanted to create a guide book for healing.

I wanted to hide behind my education and publicly-accepted experience and not share about the ambiguous and esoteric space that I operate from. I wanted to hide my less-than-perfect choices and healing from CPTSD in my messy unconventional life. I hid my identity.

Some of my greatest success has come from using the gifts I have had for lifetimes. Since age seven, I have been using the gift to see into all living beings' conditions (as I say, conflicts) and, many times, guide them and their doctors where to look and how to recover to a greater state of health. Over decades of helping individuals find the answers they needed, I've never held a business card or hung a shingle saying "Healer." But in every single part of my life and career, I was just that.

And so are you. You just might need a little clearing of your own mud on the windshield to make it easier and clearer.

From professional athletes, singer-songwriters, influencers, speakers, entrepreneur millionaires and billionaires to stay-at-home parents, I have helped others deconstruct their inner conflict and reconstruct a life that is more meaningful and fulfilling. It always unfolds organically and beautifully.

Your healing creates space for others to heal.

Writing a Book

This book has been attempting to be born for years. I kept hitting a wall. It was maddening! It wasn't until I went into a healing studio that I was shaken by the shoulders to get over myself and share myself with the world.

There was a sign on the sidewalk that said "Psychic Readings Here!" I scoffed at the sign, saying, "I don't need anyone to tell me who my twin flame is, when my lottery ticket will be bought, and when I will get married. Ha!"

But somehow, I was curious and wanted to see what the place looked like. So, I followed the sidewalk to the window that held the neon sign, *Psychic,* and saw a vortex in the middle of the room. "I want to go under that!" So, I walked in, ready to ask about the energy vortex.

Addressing the presumed owner of the store, I said "Hi, I'd like to go under the vortex."

She stared blankly at me and pointed at a chair in front of a desk. "Please, sit."

I stood.

I was not interested in a reading. I don't want to know when my twin flame is arriving, when I'll win the lottery, or will buy a new car. "I just want to go under the energy vortex."

She moved behind the desk and sat in her chair. Her bosom was falling out of her shirt, and she had a Coca-Cola can and vape at the ready.

I wrinkled my nose, thinking, *I'm not buying anything she's selling.*

She spoke again. "Please… Sit."

I sat.

I'm giving you two minutes to give me your shpiel."

"You are writing a book."

Keeping my best stone face, I said nothing.

Affirmining "Your silence allows for your spiritual presence."

She continued. "But you are afraid you'll hurt people by telling the truth."

Still staring, stone-faced, I wondered, *How does she know that? Oh. Duh. Yes, I know how. But I still don't trust her. I don't want to give anything away.* I sat silent, feeling her energy creeping into the crevices of my auric field. It felt very old, tired, and wise.

"Your story is going to save lives. There are people who are waiting for your story. They need you to write it. Your experiences and your journey are going to save lives. They are waiting for you. You are the instrument."

There it was: another one of God's messages coming from someone whom I was closed to receiving.

She stared at me while I cried. Tears jumped from the center of my bottom lids and dripped onto my lap.

Her voice monotone rattled on. "A tarot reading is $175, full-life reading $300.00, and a mini-reading $75. Are you ready for your full-life reading?"

"Well, no. Thank you. I really wanted to go under the vortex."

Apparently, the vortex was closed that day. The thing that had caught my eye wasn't available. I could have guessed but glad I didn't.

I fished in my purse for a few twenties and placed them on her white desk. Fixing my eyes on her as I stood, I nodded "Thank you" and walked out of the store.

The sun cast its light in my eyes. Looking up, I laughed at the irony of the messages we receive and from whom. *The thing we think we want isn't always the thing we need.*

Then, I pressed the start button of my BMW, rolled down the windows, and opened the sunroof as I drove off, still crying and smiling from the experience. I couldn't stop the tears from falling the whole way home. I didn't want to forget this moment. I had a knowing: "I guess it's time to finish this book."

Remembering what my shaman, ancestors, and spiritual masters had taught me, I felt deep gratitude and said out loud:

"Thank you, Angels. Thank you, universe. I am grateful for this moment."

My hope is that, by me being and sharing all of me, you feel safer to become all of you. This is my coming out party. Ta-daaaaa! What better way than to share it with you

You are a beautiful prism ready to be born. Again and again.

Prismatic Path is Ready for Your Visit

For more information on Sharon's programs to aid you on your healing journey, and to subscribe to *Thrive with Sharon* podcast on all platforms, visit:

www.SharonJeanland.com

Acknowledgments

I'm grateful beyond measure for the magic that further connected me with my daughters, created by publishing this book. My daughter Emily, who is literally on my business team and has gone above and beyond in her love and support and work. My daughter Lizzy, who has shown incredible support, sage advice, compassion, and inspiration. You both are my greatest motivation and inspiration. To have you as my two biggest believers and supporters is a gift.

To each one of my friends who let me fall apart and nurtured me back to sanity, thank you is not enough.

To my trainer, Matt, who puts *personal* in personal trainer. You understood how important it was for me to work hard and be strong, especially when I was revisiting some of my darker days. Thank you.

Though this book was created years ago, it wasn't until I met my genius publisher and now friend, Samantha Joy, who looked at me and said, "Your story needs to be told. You are writing your memoir," that it was brought to life. I'm beyond grateful for your support and love.

To my incredible clients and patients, whom I *get* to serve every day, thank you for your trust and belief in your own Healer's Journey. You are changing the world.

Most importantly, I'm grateful for the infinite capacity to heal any and all things and for the lifetimes of practice mastering this skill.

ABOUT SHARON LAND

Sharon Land is a world-class transformational guide, speaker, and holistically trained international healer/metaphysician. She has nearly twenty years of experience in high-performance coaching and mentoring, directing a multi-million-dollar business, as an entrepreneur, and blazing a trail in the healing space. Sharon is a guide to heal your past to live in full expression and freedom in all areas of your life.

Sharon's belief is that the antidote to individual and collective trauma is to provide safe spaces for healing. "We heal in safe spaces." This fuels her passion to discuss the complexities of CPTSD, mental health, healing, spirituality, somatic healing, bioscientific research, and neuroplasticity, helping other healers to understand these challenges in a way that addresses all aspects of self and wholeness. She frequently says, "We are only as strong as our weakest link." Which is why she has studied and practiced healing all aspects of the self: body, mind, spirit.

Sharon practices in the intersections of metaphysics, science, cosmic numerology, astrology, and spirituality. She is a trauma-trained holistic psychotherapist, metaphysician, and mystic. She believes the more we express all aspects of ourselves, the more we help others to heal to live abundantly, powerfully, and authentically.

At an early age, Sharon discovered her intuition and her skills, which encompass medical mediumship, distance energy testing for root-cause issues, supplement and medication alignment, biofields, past-life experiences, and soul guidance. She now uses specific protocols to address the body, mind, and spirit to return it to its intended healthy vessel.

Sharon has been featured in local and international media for her practices. She has counseled incarcerated youth, worked for the state of Tennessee to preserve the family unit, served as a director of an adult homeless shelter, on mental health advisory boards, helped create and implement a Safe Haven Community program for the homeless in New Jersey, been the national sales manager for a multimillion-dollar chemical corporation, a professional trainer and equestrian, and a serial entrepreneur.

She is a mixed-media artist, poet, writer, former professional equestrian and trainer, expressive dance facilitator, believer and supporter of ethical fair-trade practices rather than traditional consumerism, and mother of two beautiful intuitive daughters who have given her meaning behind her purpose.

Having healed from a long list of mystery illness, CPTSD, religious abuse, and narcissistic and sociopathic abuse, she is a living, breathing example of healing, transformation, and abundance. She believes in the infinite capacity of healing any and all things.

www.ingramcontent.com/pod-product-compliance
Lightning Source LLC
Chambersburg PA
CBHW031254090426
42742CB00007B/443